NICOLE ZOCH

In The Cool *Of* The Day

A collection of God-conversations, miraculous encounters and an exploration of the postures of the three Marys to abide, wait and receive.

In the Cool of the Day
Copyright 2022 ©Nicole Zoch

Published by Star Label Publishing
P.O. Box 1511, Buderim, QLD, Australia
publishing@starlabel.com.au

Editing: Jeanette Windle
Interior: Rebecca Moore
Main cover image licensed 2022 istock
Ilona Titova

1st Edition August, 2022
All rights reserved. No part of this publication may be reproduced in any form; stored in a retrieval system; or transmitted; or used in any other form; or by any other means without prior written permission of the publisher (except for brief quotes for the purpose of review or promotion).

All Scripture quotations unless otherwise indicated are from The Holy Bible, New International Version®, NIV® Copyright © 1973, 1978, 1984, 2011 by Biblica, Inc.™ Used by permission. All rights reserved worldwide.

Scripture quotations marked TPT are from The Passion Translation®. Copyright © 2017, 2018 by Passion & Fire Ministries, Inc. Used by permission. All rights reserved. ThePassionTranslation.com.

Scripture quotations marked MSG are taken from The Message. Copyright © 1993, 1994, 1995, 1996, 2000, 2001, 2002. Used by permission of NavPress Publishing Group.

Scripture quotations marked AMP are taken from the Amplified® Bible (AMP), Copyright © 2015 by The Lockman Foundation, Used by permission. www.Lockman.org.

Scripture quotations marked (NLT) are taken from the Holy Bible, New Living Translation, copyright © 1996, 2004, 2007 by Tyndale House Foundation. Used by permission of Tyndale House Publishers, Inc., Carol Stream, IL 60188. All rights reserved.

Scripture taken from the New King James Version®. Copyright © 1982 by Thomas Nelson, Inc. Used by permission. All rights reserved.

The views expressed here-in remain the sole responsibility of the author, who exempts the publisher from all liability. The author and publisher do not assume responsibility for any loss, damage, or disruption caused by the contents, errors or omissions, whether such contents, errors, or omissions result from opinion, negligence, accident, or any other cause, and hereby disclaim any and all liability to any party.

ISBN: 978-0-6453697-1-7

FOR HIM ALONE

Each day as I walk and talk with my Father in heaven, I journal all that I learn by being in His presence. As I position myself to abide in Him, as I lean in close and wait on Him to receive, I am constantly amazed at what God chooses to reveal. *In The Cool Of The Day* is the result of many of my early morning God-conversations.

So it is my wonderful Lord and Saviour Jesus that I thank first and foremost for gifting me the opportunity to share our heart-to-hearts through this book. God is the only reason I write. An audience with the King is all I desire. And so I write for Him. I write because of Him. I write to honour Him.

To my heavenly Father, may these words I have scribed be like an aroma of sweet essence. As I write of God's love and faithfulness, may I convey just a portion of the indescribable love our Father has for each of His sons and daughters. May the God-moments I share in this book, along with the testimonies of Mary of Bethany, Mary Magdalene, and Mary the mother of Jesus, encourage all of us to *abide, wait,* and *receive* as we seek to hear the voice of God for ourselves.

THANK YOU

A book cannot be written without the support of many. It requires a team around it to accomplish its purpose. I would like to acknowledge and thank several people for journeying with me in producing *In The Cool Of The Day*.

Firstly and most importantly to my husband Jamie and three children, Faith, Joel, and Levi, thank you for your loving patience and for gifting me the much needed time and space to complete this project. I love that you see this as my calling as much as I do. I thank each of you for cheering me on in your own special way.

Thank you, Jamie, for always being my greatest confidant and for always knowing just what I need at exactly the right time like the numerous writing retreats down by the beach you booked for me, knowing I was struggling to find solace in the busyness of life at home. I am incredibly blessed by your godly discernment and your generous heart.

Thank you also for being my personal life coach, a testament of your teacher/shepherd gifts from which I benefit enormously. Pearls of wisdom you offer in our early morning talks and prayers regularly end up framing my God-conversations later that morning. God has certainly gifted you with wisdom and discernment, and I am so blessed to have you as my soul partner.

To my most precious daughter Faith, the firstborn of our faith journey so many moons ago, thank you for being my number-one encourager. How many times have you sat and listened to me practice a preaching message or willingly re-read one of my chapters? You are such a treasure to me, truly a gift from heaven. I watch as you grow into a beautiful, courageous young warrior for Jesus. You have the law of God etched on your heart (Jeremiah 31:33), and being a true advocate of justice is already a strong motivator in your life choices. I know God has amazing plans for your life, and I am already your number-one fan. You make me swell with pride, and I can't wait, my beautiful daughter, to witness what God does in and through you in the years to come.

To Joel, my soulful, reflective one. I love the many times you have asked about my God-moments, wanting me to share with you the conversations I've had with my heavenly Father. An echo of the prophetic in you as well, I truly believe. I think my favourite request was the day you asked if you could join me on one of my prayer walks just so you could meet and talk with God in person as well. My son, I promise you that God is available to all of us. Take your own walk with God. He is waiting for you. He longs to chat with you as a friend face-to-face (Exodus 33:11). You are His precious son. You are mine as well.

And to my Levi, we have such a special bond. I love how you see God in situations and events, always questioning whether God has orchestrated something behind the scenes for our protection or provision. I love how you have often asked about the miraculous moments that have framed my life story and which I write about in this book. I encourage you, my beloved son, to keep on seeking because the more you seek, the more you will find the answers (Jeremiah 29:13). That is in fact what a relationship with God is all about, and He is longing to share His mysteries with you. Our Father in heaven delights in you, my darling child, and so do I.

I also want to acknowledge others outside my immediate family. Behind every good book is an awesome team, and I have the best! So firstly, I want to give credit to my amazing editor. Thank you Jeanette Windle for once again polishing my work so beautifully. As with my first book *Having Faith,* Jeanette, you have captured the true essence of my heart's desire and reworked my words to reflect God's glory more accurately. You are an editor wonder, and I am so fortunate to have your expertise on my team.

To my friend and fellow author Rebecca Moore and her team from Star Label Publishing, thank you for partnering with me in publishing this book. You have captured my thoughts and imagination beautifully in the cover and internal design, and I thank God for your creativity.

And to my readers, thank you for your fellowship and support. I am grateful for the many who have urged my writing on and encouraged me when I was struggling to put pen to paper. I am grateful I can write to bless and inspire you to pursue Jesus above all else. You are His beloved. May He always be yours.

DEDICATION

To Jamie, my best friend and husband of twenty-seven years. You are my rock and the love of my life. Even in life's storms, you have always remained solid and steadfast. Like a tower of strength, you have not wavered even for a moment. You are such an inspiration to me, and I am truly grateful that God has gifted me with such a partner who seeks after wisdom and truth and who is selfless in his pursuit to ensure our needs are always met. You are everything to me, and this book is dedicated to you, my one and only life-long love.

Contents

Foreword 1

In The Cool Of The Day 5

Poem Of My Heart – A New Day Dawns 7

Introduction – Cuppa With My Papa 9

It's Where I Belong 15

Song Of My Heart 16

Chapter 1 – The Shepherd's Voice 19

Chapter 2 – God's Communication Methods 27

Chapter 3 – Revelation-Secrets 35

Mary Posture – Abide – Lesson #1 42

Present In His Presence 43

Devotion Of My Heart – The Essence of Being in His Presence 44

Chapter 4 – The Present 47

Chapter 5 – Perfectly Imperfect 57

Chapter 6 – No Story God Can't Redeem 65

Mary Posture – Abide – Lesson #2 73

Queen In Waiting 74

Devotion of My Heart – An Audience With The King ... 75

Chapter 7 – Season Of Waiting 77

Chapter 8 – Not My Will But Yours 87

Chapter 9 – Opened Door..93

Mary Posture – Wait – Lesson #3......................................98

What's In Your Hand?..99

Devotion Of My Heart – Ordinary to Extraordinary.........100

Chapter 10 – Mountain Goat..101

Chapter 11 – God Waits Too...109

Mary Posture – Wait – Lesson #4....................................115

I Am Who Christ Says I Am!...116

Devotion Of My Heart
   – The Transforming Power Of God's Glory.................117

Chapter 12 – Identity...119

Chapter 13 – Power Of The Tongue...............................127

Mary Posture – Receive – Lesson #5...............................135

Then One Day..136

Devotion Of My Heart – Our Father At Work Everyday...137

Chapter 14 – God Encounters...139

Chapter 15 – God Of The Eleventh Hour........................147

Mary Posture – Abide, Wait, and Receive – Lesson #6....151

Unveiled For More Of His Glory.....................................152

Devotion Of My Heart – More Of Your Glory.................153

Chapter 16 – Mount Sinai Encounter Sanctuary.............155

Chapter 17 – Torn In Two...163

Chapter 18 – Greater Measure.......................................171

Mary Posture – Abide, Wait, and Receive – Lesson #7..................176

New Bridal Dance..................177

Lyrics Of My Heart – Oh Love Divine, How Sweet Thou Art..........178

Chapter 19 – Dance Of Intimacy..................179

Chapter 20 – Dance Of Unison..................189

Chapter 21 – Extravagant Love..................199

Mary Posture – Abide, Wait, and Receive – Lesson #8..................208

Beginning To End..................209

Prayer Of My Heart..................210

Chapter 22 – Family Heirloom..................211

Chapter 23 – Herald The Revelation..................219

Chapter 24 – Testify Of His Goodness..................225

Final Exhortation..................233

Devotion Of My Heart – On God Assignment..................234

Epilogue..................237

Appendix..................241

About The Author..................243

FOREWORD

Some people come into your life, and you know it was by the hand of God. Nicole and I live on opposite ends of Australia—Nicole in Victoria, myself in Queensland—yet when God wants to connect people, no amount of distance is ever too far.

When Nicole's first book *Having Faith* and my second book *Pizza & Choir* were released in 2019, a picture was posted to Instagram of Nicole standing in front of the Blackburn Koorong new release stand. As I browsed at the new releases on the shelf, I noticed my own book displayed near hers. Out of the blue, and as a complete stranger to her, I contacted Nicole to congratulate her and to share publishing stories. I guess my excitement got the better of me. We became instant friends, swapping books and meeting on occasion when in each other's cities.

While reading *Having Faith*, I was amazed to see how many important dates and places matched those in my own life, and we had no doubt crossed paths in the past without knowledge of it at the time.

On meeting Nicole, I knew she was a daughter of God who relished being in His presence. Immediately our conversations went straight to Scripture and what God was doing in the world and in the lives of us and those around us. We talked for hours and, though we don't often see each other due to distance, these are conversations that are picked up with ease when circumstances allow.

God-ordained friendships are a blessing beyond measure and prove to be an encouragement and support that God knows His daughters need. Since meeting Nicole, I have continued to be encouraged and strengthened by her prophetic words as her God-given gift has continued to be fanned into a bright and shining flame.

When Nicole asked me to publish her book through Star Label Publishing, I was both honoured and excited. Honoured, knowing that she was entrusting me to package and deliver the words God had placed on her heart to the world, and excited, to read the words and revelation God had been pouring into her heart over these past months. I was certainly not disappointed.

Nicole speaks straight to the heart of God's sons and daughters, speaking His words in a way that is essential for the days we are living in. She communicates the Father's love with grace, gentleness, and a longing for His children to be in intimate conversation with Him, while also preparing them to be ready for His glorious return. Jesus is so looking forward to gathering His Bride to Him, and those who wait expectantly are excited too. It will be a wonderful marriage feast!

Nicole's inspired work *In the Cool of the Day* is like eating fruit—nourishing for the soul—and will inspire fruitfulness within its readers. Every child of God who longs to be in His presence, to know Him more, and to be hearing His beautiful voice, should read this book. It is certainly a book that is birthed for such a time as this. I recommend it for every son, daughter, mother, father, grandmother, grandfather, friend, and for those seeking the love of a close friend and Father who will never let them down.

In the Cool of the Day

I no longer call you servants, because a servant does not know his master's business. Instead, I have called you friends, for everything that I learned from my Father I have made known to you. You did not choose me, but I chose you and appointed you so that you might go and bear fruit—fruit that will last—and so that whatever you ask in my name the Father will give you.

(John 15:15-16 NIV)

Rebecca Moore
Publisher
Star Label Publishing

I have known Nicole and Jamie for over twenty-five and forty-five years respectively. Having grown up in the same exclusive church denomination, in later life we all experienced a new found freedom in who and what Jesus Christ really is, and how to have a deep, and personal relationship with Him.

Throughout the pages of *In The Cool Of The Day*, Nicole definitively establishes from Scripture the spiritual principles of *abiding, waiting* and *receiving*, and through revelation and insights from the Spirit of God, she unpacks them thoroughly and considerately.

Using real life application and experiences, Nicole teaches us how to enjoy a greater relationship with the triune God. You will be blessed by reading this book—your faith will be strengthened, and you will be encouraged to spend more time in His loving presence.

Leanne Shaw
Co-Senior Pastor - Living Faith Community Church, Perth, Western Australia

In the Cool of the Day

In the morning, Lord, you hear my voice; in the morning I lay my requests before you and wait expectantly.
—Psalm 5:3

POEM OF MY HEART

A New Day Dawns

With every morning sunlight ray,
A new day dawns, come what may,
And as I choose to pause and pray,
This, my Lord, is what I say:

"With all my heart, I long for this:
To know You more and to dwell by Your side.
With all my heart I desire this:
To receive Your love and to feel Your touch.
With all my heart I search for this:
To know I am Yours and to know You are mine."

And so with every new sun ray,
I promise, Lord, to come and pray.
And as I heed Your voice each day,
By Your side is where I'll stay.

—By Nicole Zoch

INTRODUCTION

Let the dawning day bring me revelation of your tender, unfailing love. Give me light for my path and teach me, for I trust in you.

—Psalm 143:8 TPT

I am a morning person. I always have been, and I'm sure I always will be. I love waking up to the sound of birds and the hum of nature as it slowly rouses from its night-time slumber. I love watching as the stars and moon begin to disappear and the sun rises over the horizon as if to proudly declare a new day has dawned.

I have even noticed in recent years that it is early in the morning when most galactic activities seem to be visible. In those pre-sunrise hours when I lay awake in bed gazing out our east-facing window and enjoying the expanse of the heavens, I am often privy to numerous shooting stars. It is as if the galaxy is awakening, alive and bursting with energy.

I love it when our family chooses to holiday close to the ocean somewhere along our vast Australian coastline. I relish dipping my feet into the cool, salty water and squishing my toes in the moist, white sand, watching and praying as the day slowly unfolds over the South Pacific Ocean.

I am usually at my most joyous at the break of dawn, although these days it takes a strong shot of caffeine to get me going. What seemed to bother me the night before is often inconsequential by morning, as a song written by King David reminds me.

> Weeping may stay for the night, but rejoicing comes in the morning. (Psalm 30:5)

At daybreak, I am usually well awake and fully ready for the day ahead. So it's no surprise that I also choose to *abide, wait,* and *receive* from my Creator God in the early morning. In our region, this is 'the cool' of my day, just as Scripture describes how God walked and talked with Adam and Eve 'in the cool of the day' (Genesis 3:8).

It was actually during one of these early morning walks and talks with God several years back that I felt the Spirit of God ask me to start writing down our conversations. I say conversations because that is exactly what spending time in God's presence looks like to me. I need it to be a two-way exchange. I never want it to be a monologue where I do all the talking and I never pause long enough to listen. I need to hear from God. I want to be invited into His plan and purpose for my life, and I don't want to miss a thing.

A friend of mine describes her morning time with God as having a cup of coffee with Him. Just two besties hanging out and chatting. "A cuppa with my Papa" is how I like to put it.

My morning dates with my heavenly Papa revolve more around walking and talking, although coffee in hand would actually go down a treat. But it is the many wonderful discussions I've had and continue to enjoy with my heavenly Father in the cool of my day that I want to share with you in this book.

I also want to explore what I like to call the Mary postures of *abiding, waiting,* and *receiving,* which Mary of Bethany, Mary Magdalene, and Mary the mother of Jesus chose to take. I hope that these three Marys, of whom we will learn more throughout this book, will inspire each of us to abide at the feet of Jesus (Mary of Bethany), patiently wait for His instruction (Mary Magdalene), and receive God's calling on our life (Mary the mother of Jesus).

As we unpack the spiritual truths gleaned from the testimonies of these three Marys along with my own heart-to-heart conversations with the Father, I hope and pray that the Spirit of God will stir something deep within your heart and reveal more of Himself to you as well. My sincere desire as we journey this book together, as we abide, wait, and receive along the way, is that each one of us will choose to passionately seek the Father, zealously pursue all He has for us, and that all of us will choose to walk and talk with Him in the cool of our very own day, whatever and whenever that looks like.

To this end, I will share occasionally throughout the following pages an additional word of encouragement, prayer of hope, declaration of God's love, or message of joy. I believe this is what the Father wants to offer each of His children through this book. Almost every sentence I've written is the result of my abiding with, waiting on, and receiving from God. I have simply written whatever I felt the Spirit of God say to me, and I want to share some of those conversations with you throughout this book. What I hope to achieve through my writing is an openness to what the Spirit is sharing with me that will encourage your walk with God as well.

Sometimes what I share will come in a form of reproach or reprimand toward myself. If I am to be open and honest on the pages ahead, I need to be vulnerable. So you will learn of my brokenness as well as the anxieties and fears that have sometimes overwhelmed me. In that, I think you will see similarities to our three Marys as well.

You will also see me rise, fall, then get back up, ready to go again. You will hear my heartfelt cries as well as my songs of jubilation. You will learn of a daughter of the King who is desperately seeking the plans God has for me.

As I share this collection of what I've experienced on my morning walks, I hope you will see that walking and talking with God is always a truthful experience. One that takes you through the valleys, up to the mountain tops, and then back down again.

A spiritual journey isn't all highs, and it shouldn't

be all lows either. The great evangelist Billy Graham was once quoted as saying:

> The Christian life is not a constant high. I have my moments of deep discouragement. I have to go to God in prayer with tears in my eyes, and say, "O God, forgive me, or help me."

In that, I think Mary the mother of Jesus could have also testified to the ebbs and flows of life that can be enthralling and enlightening but challenging and heart-breaking as well. It is this mix of highs and lows that makes our journey so real. To be in God's presence regardless of what season we are faced with is what a true relationship with the Father is all about.

So, dear friends, I invite you to come along on my morning walks. Enter into my private conversations with God. Join me in the following pages as we listen to what the Spirit of God wants to share through the Marys.

Let me also encourage you to pause along the way as I've done so often along my morning walks. Many times I've found a log, hill, or bridge, somewhere to sit and listen, ponder, and take in all that the Father wanted to impart.

God wants to talk to us, so as you read my God-conversations, as you take your own Mary postures, take the time to question what the Spirit might want you to learn along the way. What message might Jesus want to convey to you personally?

Consider your own journey, the times in your life that have been marked by God-moments. Reflect on those times where you've known absolutely that Jesus has spoken directly into a situation. Ponder the times you've thought something was coincidental rather than spiritual. Was it really? Or was God working tirelessly in the background of your life at that moment?

If talking to and hearing from God is new for you, I will show you throughout this book how it can be as natural as any other earthly relationship. More so since it is what we've been created to enjoy. Relationship with our Father in heaven is in our design, our make-up, our DNA. After all, we are His sons and daughters made in His glorious image as God Himself stated when we were first created.

> So God created mankind in his own image, in the image of God he created them; male and female he created them. (Genesis 1:27)

So, dear readers, are you willing to go on a journey of discovery? Are you ready to walk and talk with God in the cool of your day? Will you posture yourselves like the three Marys, willing to abide, wait, and receive?

It's where I Belong

[Martha] had a sister named Mary who seated herself at the Lord's feet, and was continually listening to his teachings.
—Luke 10:39 AMP

SONG OF MY HEART

It's Where I Belong

Verse 1

Under Your wings, I rest.

Close by Your side, I walk.

To sit at Your feet, to know You are near,

It's where I belong.

Verse 2

Bathed in Your glorious light,

Washed in Your righteous blood,

To feel Your embrace, to know I am loved,

It's where I belong.

Chorus

So speak to me, God, teach me Your ways.

Show me the plans You have for me; teach me to pray.

I'm here to stay, gazed at Your face.

To hear from the One, it's where I belong.

Bridge

Under Your wings, close by Your side, sitting at Your feet,

Bathed in Your light, washed by Your blood, held in Your arms,

I know that's where I belong.

End

To hear from the One,

It's where I belong.

—By Nicole Zoch, Copyright 2018

CHAPTER ONE

The Shepherd's Voice

> My sheep listen to my voice; I know them, and they follow me.
>
> —John 10:27

I can't seem to go very long without being in God's presence. Whenever I prolong spending time with Him, my weaknesses begin to overwhelm me. Sin creeps in, and the old selfish, vain, insecure me emerges. I'm always surprised at how quickly my old self breaks through. So very close to the surface my old ways clearly remain!

I hope I'm not the exception here. Maybe I am. But what I've come to recognise, at least in my own life, is that of and by my own strength I can do nothing but return to self. The old flesh stirs and tries to rise. It appears time and time again. But when I remain close to my Lord, when I seek His face and sit at His feet, as Mary of Bethany's story in Luke 10 teaches us (more about her story later),

I can do as the apostle Paul describes in his letter to the church of Philippi.

> For I can do everything through Christ, who gives me strength. (Philippians 4:13 NLT)

Experiencing God in an intimate way has been something I've sought all my life. If you've read *Having Faith*, a book I wrote about my nine-year barrenness-to-motherhood journey, you will know that intimacy with God was very much a part of my healing process. If I hadn't spent quality time in His presence, listening, learning, receiving, and moving in His timing, I might have missed out on all God was doing in my life. I needed deliverance from personal issues, matrimonial hurts, spiritual wounds, and a barren womb.

Restoration in all these areas of my life came about because of a wonderful, close relationship I had formed with my Creator God. Intimacy with the Trinity of God was the greatest gift that came out of my barren condition. The second was a by-product of the first, which was the gift of mothering my three beautiful children.

Even as a child I wanted to know God more deeply. Talking with Him about every aspect of my life felt the most natural part of my existence. I grew up in a church that taught predominantly only from the teachings of the Old Testament Mosaic law, so my understanding of God was mostly centred around the Old Covenant rather than the New. But despite my limited understanding of who He is, I loved God the Father ever so passionately. My

The Shepherd's Voice

relationship with my heavenly Father was very real and personal to me, even though the triune nature of God was not revealed to me until I was well into my twenties.

In 2017, Jamie and I and our children were living on a farm in Victoria, Australia's southernmost state except for the island of Tasmania. I was walking early one morning along the kangaroo tracks that indented the grounds of our farm when God brought to my mind childhood memories of my relationship with Him. As I trekked along, breathing in the familiar therapeutic aroma of the eucalyptus trees that are so prevalent in Victoria's countryside, I was reminded of the many encounters I'd had even as a young girl where God spoke into a situation.

I suddenly realised that my walking and talking with God was not something new for me. It is in fact who I am. It has always been part of my every day. It has framed my entire life.

One particular memory God reminded me of on that trek bears witness to my hearing and following God's voice. The memory was of a day that has often reminded me how I can indeed trust in the voice of my Shepherd. It was the day God saved my life from being struck by lightning. A moment where God directly and almost audibly spoke to me.

I say almost audibly because the voice in my head was louder than any sounds I could hear around me. So while I don't think I literally heard God speaking audibly on that day, internally I understood that the direction I received was very definitely and clearly from Him.

I was about fourteen years old at the time and

living with my family in Queensland, a state in northern Australia's tropical zone. It was a typical stormy afternoon of northern Australia's wet season, which runs from December through April. I'd just returned home from school and was sitting on a lounge chair in our family living room, mulling over what I would do for the rest of the afternoon. My mother was in her room, my dad out of the house, my two older brothers most likely raiding the fridge as they did most afternoons upon returning home from school.

I must have decided on my afternoon activities because it was the exact moment I began to get up off the chair when I heard God's voice telling me quite urgently to sit back down and do so quickly. Without any mental debate, I immediately acted on that directive.

Just as I sat back down, lightning pierced through the windows of our family's living room, skimming over my head. The lightning proceeded to bounce from one light fixture to another until all the light bulbs in the room exploded. Had I still been standing, that lightning bolt would have struck my body, most likely killing me instantly.

So, you see, I've known my Shepherd's voice from as young as I can remember. This shouldn't surprise me or anyone reading this. After all, Jesus reminds us:

> My sheep listen to my voice; I know them, and they follow me. (John 10:27)

The Shepherd's Voice

Still, it has only been in recent years I've realised that I've been listening to and following the voice of Jesus for my entire life. The above words of Jesus have been my literal walk. They have framed my existence as naturally as I breathe. I talk to God. I expect Him to talk to me in return. And so I follow His lead.

I don't know if this makes my walk unique. Or do others as they ponder their life journey and consider the inner whispers that frame their decision-making and thought life also recognise this is God talking to His children? I see it in my own children's walk, times when a divine intervention has occurred and my kids can either see it as a coincidence or identify it as a God-moment. I am grateful to witness them more often than not choosing the latter.

I've had this confirmed through my parents, husband, friends who've encountered a whisper of caution, internal applause of encouragement, reprimand tugging on the heartstrings, a Scripture that seems written directly for their current situation. These are God-conversations. God revealing His love for His children. God relating to us.

As I keep on walking and talking with God along the kangaroo prints of my country hillside, I am reminded of another God-moment in my life. This time it was God intervening to save the life of my firstborn and only daughter Faith. While not a verbal direction on this occasion, God nevertheless demonstrated His plan for Faith's life very tangibly.

Faith would have only been weeks old at the time I happened to be standing at a busy intersection, waiting to cross the road. I'd just finished doing some shopping, and in a sleep-deprived instance of early motherhood, I absentmindedly started to cross the road. But I'd failed to notice a car heading directly for the pram in which Faith lay peacefully.

Just before imminent impact, someone grabbed my body, swinging me back onto the footpath with such ferocity it also pulled the pram cradling my daughter up onto the curb. Neither of us was harmed. In fact, Faith continued in blissful ignorance.

The driver who'd narrowly missed hitting the pram beeped and yelled profanities at me in sheer panic as the vehicle turned the corner. I too was shaken and panicked as it dawned on me what had nearly happened. My daughter, whose birth I'd awaited and prayed for nine full years, had almost been taken from me through one moment of absentmindedness.

Tearfully, I turned around to thank, hug, and cry over whoever had just saved Faith's life. Instead, I stood there shocked. No other person was there. In fact, I couldn't see a single other person walking anywhere nearby. God had instead spoken through His actions. He wasn't finished with my daughter just yet. He still had a plan and purpose for her life on this earth. There had been no time to tell me to move backward. So He'd needed to physically step in and move me miraculously.

Fifteen years later, I can still see God's hand mightily on my daughter's life. She is in His design, and the purpose for which she was created will be for His glory and His honour. I wait excitedly to see God's plan for the next phase of Faith's life.

Another similar instance of God stepping in miraculously to save the day occurred a year or so before my daughter was born. On this occasion, it was me who needed to be rescued. My husband Jamie loves to ride dirt-bikes. We'd formed a great friendship circle with others in our church family who shared his passion. On one occasion, we all headed to a mutual friend's property that had a quarry on which they'd built a motocross circuit.

I'd never ridden a dirt-bike before, so I thought I'd test out one of the bikes by riding it up to the top of the quarry. Jamie had given me a briefing on how to ride the bike, and it seemed easy enough. As my confidence grew, so did my speed.

There was only one problem. Jamie had forgotten to show me where the brake was. As I neared the top of the quarry, I had no idea how to stop the bike. I was heading straight off the cliff, and there was nothing I could do to stop it.

Inches from the edge, I did the only thing I knew to do. I cried out to Jesus to save me. Immediately, the bike turned off on its own. With my tire on the very edge of the quarry drop-off and my dumbfounded gaze looking down over the gully, I was completely shaken. But for God's intervention, my life would have been taken from me due to a hasty, unprepared decision. Suffice it to say I've never been keen to ride a dirt bike ever since!

CHAPTER TWO

God's Communication Methods

For God speaks again and again . . . he speaks in dreams, in visions of the night . . . [and] he whispers in their ears.

—Job 33:14-16 NLT

I love that God still communicates with His children today. The life-saving stories I shared in the previous chapter are testament to this. God desires an intimate relationship with each one of us. Throughout Scripture, there is evidence of God communicating with His people in all sorts of ways. Nothing has changed. He still wants to relate to us today.

I also love that God's communication methods are sometimes unconventional, even radical. He spoke to Moses through a non-extinguishing burning bush (Exodus 3).

Later, Moses spent time in God's presence on Mount Sinai, where God gave Moses His law for the people of Israel, including the Ten Commandments. When Moses descended from the mountain, he radiated the glory of God so brightly from being in God's presence that no one could look upon his face for some time (Exodus 34:29-30).

That's not even the most bizarre way God has communicated with humans. How about the time God spoke through a donkey to get the attention of a prophet named Balaam, who because of that encounter would eventually speak "only what God puts in [his] mouth" (Numbers 22:21-39). Yes, our Creator is indeed the God of 'out of the box' as God's words to the prophet Isaiah reminds us.

> "For my thoughts are not your thoughts, neither are your ways my ways," declares the Lord. (Isaiah 55:8)

God reveals Himself as He needs to. Sometimes God speaks through visions and dreams. We see God communicating this way many times to Old Testament patriarchs, judges, and prophets, ordinary farmers like Gideon (Judges 6:11-27), maidservants like Hagar (Genesis 21: 6-19), even women struggling as I did with infertility like Samson's mother (Judges 13:3-5) and Isaac's wife Rebekah (Genesis 25:23).

Sometimes God spoke through angelic visitations such as when the archangel Gabriel told Mary she would bear the Messiah (Luke 1:26-38). Other times, people were moved from one location to another as I experienced

God's Communication Methods

when God saved Faith and me from that oncoming vehicle. Philip, one of the twelve disciples, experienced this after his evangelistic encounter with the Ethiopian eunuch.

> When they came up out of the water, the Spirit of the Lord snatched Philip away. The eunuch never saw him again but went on his way rejoicing. Meanwhile, Philip found himself farther north at the town of Azotus. He preached the Good News there and in every town along the way until he came to Caesarea. (Acts 8:39-40 NLT)

An even more dramatic example of being moved to another location was when the apostle Paul was taken up into the third heaven and shown many extraordinary things from God (2 Corinthians 12). John, the 'beloved disciple' and author of the last book of the Bible, was also taken up into heaven (Revelation 4:1-2), where he experienced many prophetic visions that he penned for all to read (Revelation 1-22).

The Bible records other unconventional methods of God communicating with His people. Things like God muting Zechariah for his disbelief that his wife Elizabeth, who had been barren for a very long time, would become pregnant with John the Baptist (Luke 1:20). God blinded Saul, now known as the apostle Paul, along the road to Damascus to gain Paul's attention, avert his aggressive, murderous actions against the followers of Jesus, and redirect him into his God-given purpose and calling (Acts 9:1-22). So many extraordinary, interesting, even challenging to our sensibilities encounters with the God of the universe!

But in fact, humanity was designed from the beginning of time to commune with God and He with us. Adam and Eve walking and talking with God in the cool of their day (Genesis 3:8) were not the exception but the example for all of us.

And God still wants to commune with all of us. The Garden of Eden was supposed to be our home, and that home includes a relationship with our Creator. When considering all the different people to whom God spoke throughout biblical history, not one was so holy that they should qualify for God to speak to them more than to any of us today.

God does not discriminate based on how good or how bad we think we are. He doesn't hold us back because of our gender or even how old or how young we might be. After all, the mother of Jesus was a young Jewish girl, quite possibly as young as the tender age of thirteen when her calling was first birthed since that was not an uncommon age for marriage among the poorer classes of especially first century Israel.

You see, we are all God's most beloved. God sees His children as being one in Christ Jesus (Galatians 3:27-29). If God's attention was based on our good works, behaviour, or anything else, not one of us would deserve a moment of His consideration. Thankfully, God doesn't make that distinction as the apostle Paul, a one-time violent murderer and persecutor of God's followers, explains.

God's Communication Methods

> For it is by grace you have been saved, through faith
> - and this is not from yourselves, it is the gift of God
> - not by works, so that no one can boast. (Ephesians 2:8-9)

If God wants to talk with His children and if Scripture reveals this to be so throughout human history, how then do we press in to hear His voice better? How do we learn to hear our Shepherd's voice more clearly?

Let's start with the first of the three Mary postures I want to share with you in this book—*abiding*. For me personally, abiding at the feet of Jesus as well as abiding in His Word (John 8:31) has been and continues to be the primary stance I take for hearing the voice of God. In truth, abiding in Jesus and abiding in His Word is one and the same. There is no separation as the Gospel of John makes clear.

> In the beginning was the Word and the Word was with God, and the Word was God. The Word became flesh and made his dwelling among us. We have seen his glory, the glory of the one and only Son, who came from the Father, full of grace and truth. (John 1:1, 14)

When we experience an intimate union with Jesus, the Word made flesh, a growing bond and trust in Him is established. And through regular abiding and reading of His Word, which is God-breathed and given by divine inspiration (2 Timothy 3:16), our confidence in hearing our Shepherd's voice will become more fine-tuned.

In my own experience, once my air-wave frequency

has been attuned to what the Spirit of God is wanting to say to me, the second two Mary postures—patiently *waiting* for God's further instruction and *receiving* His directive—have been easier to accept and follow. More on these two postures later. But in terms of hearing the voice of God more accurately in our own lives, abiding close to the Spirit of God is the only way. There is no other 'magic formula'.

As I've already mentioned, one biblical personage highly esteemed for her posture of abiding is Mary, one of two sisters who lived in the town of Bethany (Luke 10). Mary of Bethany makes up the first of our three Marys. She is renowned for sitting at the feet of Jesus on three separate occasions. This makes her a perfect example of someone who values the posture of abiding in Jesus's presence, choosing to listen and learn from her Master, despite some familiar opposition.

We will look at Mary of Bethany's second and third occasions of abiding in later chapters. But in Mary's first 'abiding' experience that we are given in Scripture, Jesus and His disciples are being hosted at the home of Mary and her sister Martha. It was during this first encounter that Mary chose to abide at the feet of Jesus, savouring all that her Teacher chose to impart despite her sister Martha's annoyance.

> As Jesus and his disciples were on their way, he came to a village where a woman named Martha opened her home to him. She had a sister called Mary, who sat at the Lord's feet listening to what he said. But Martha was distracted

by all the preparations that had to be made. She came to him and asked, "Lord don't you care that my sister has left me to do the work by myself? Tell her to help me. "Martha, Martha", the Lord answered, "you are worried and upset about many things, but few things are needed – or indeed only one. Mary has chosen what is better, and it will not be taken away from her." (Luke 10:38-42)

Here are two sisters with very different postures. One was busy working towards pleasing Jesus, making preparations for feeding and housing her guests. The other knew where she belonged—at the feet of her Lord—and was content just to sit there and listen to His every word. While Martha busied herself in duty, becoming more frustrated by the minute at her sister's seemingly lazy disposition, Mary understood the value of abiding in Jesus's presence, devouring His teachings, gleaning all that she could as she sat waiting at her Master's feet.

Mary's posture suggests she wasn't concerned about the day's chores. On this occasion, the dishes could wait, the floors could go without a sweep, and dinner could be late coming. Resisting the need to work or prepare a meal, Mary made the better choice to seat herself on the floor beside Jesus and feed instead off the 'bread of life' as Jesus describes Himself.

> I am the bread of life. Whoever comes to me will never go hungry, and whoever believes in me will never be thirsty. (John 6:35)

This was where Mary belonged. It's actually where Martha belonged too. She just couldn't see it at the time. Abiding needs to be our everyday posture as well if we want to learn how to hear the voice of God more clearly in our own lives. Because, as we will see next, there are 'revelation-secrets of His promises' (Psalm 25:14 TPT) that the Lord wants to share with His devoted, those who choose to abide at His feet.

CHAPTER THREE

There's a private place reserved for the devoted lovers of [Jesus], where they sit near him and receive the revelation-secrets of his promises.

—Psalm 25:14 TPT

It may sound cliché to say that the more time you spend in God's presence, the more attuned you will become to hearing His voice. But Jesus reiterated this very truth when speaking to His disciples the last night He spent with them before going to the cross.

> He who abides in me, and I in him, bears much fruit; for without me you can do nothing . . . If you abide in me, and my words abide in you, you will ask what you desire, and it shall be done for you. (John 15:5,7 NKJV)

According to my Google thesaurus, to abide means to follow, hold onto, dwell with, entwine ourselves in, remain by the side of, be of one accord, unite, and bond together. These are words that describe an intimate relationship not so dissimilar to a marriage union. Such a union is first described directly following God's creation of Eve as Adam's spouse.

> A man shall leave his father and his mother, and be joined ["cleave" in some translations] to his wife, and they shall become one flesh. (Genesis 2:24 NKJV)

In other words, our abiding with God is also a deeply intimate connection that requires time, effort, and even cleaving to grow the relationship. This is something I know a little about from my own courting years. Jamie and I first started dating in 1993. I was living then in Queensland's capital city of Brisbane in northern Australia while Jamie resided in the countryside of Victoria, the most southern state of mainland Australia. You can read more about our dating and early marriage years in *Having Faith*. But during those early courting years, our worlds were nearly two thousand kilometres apart.

Maintaining a long-distance relationship in the 1990s was no mean feat. It had its communication challenges, that's for sure! Jamie and I would try to spend as much time conversing as we could. But for those of you who lived through the 1990s, you will remember that mobile phones and other media devices were not readily available. Most social media platforms had not yet been invented. That meant no Facetime, Snap Chat, Zoom, or any kind of face-to-face or immediate contact other than in-person visits.

I know this may seem like a life sentence, especially in today's culture of instant messaging. But I promise you we did manage to get by. During this long-distance courting season, Jamie and I used old-fashioned snail-mail to write to one another. We also called about once a week—and on a landline at that.

Domestic flights were costly, so we visited in person only a few times in that first year especially. The first day or so back together was always more than a little awkward. There was nervous tension between us and often uncomfortable politeness as we struggled to synchronise and get used to being in each other's physical presence again. In truth, it took a lot of hard and intentional work.

The same thing can happen when we keep God at a distance. If we don't spend much time in the Lord's presence, if our abiding is infrequent or only ever occasional, we have to constantly re-get-to-know Him. We have to re-learn to hear the Spirit's voice and to feel comfortable in Jesus's presence.

During my long-distance relationship with Jamie, we had to *become* in sync with each other, rather than simply *be* in sync. The first requires working towards synchronisation. The other is a current state of being.

The same can happen with an occasional relationship with God. But the good news for you and me is that despite our absence that can cause us to get out of sync with Him, God remains constantly in alignment with us. God is unchanging (Hebrews 13:8). In fact, Jesus tells us that our heavenly Father knows what we need when we need it well before we even ask for it (Matthew 6:8). That's how in-sync our loving Father is towards us, His beloved children.

Jamie and I have now been married for twenty-seven years, and we rarely stay apart for any length of time. In consequence, we will frequently share the same thoughts and often finish each other's sentences. Since we spend a lot of time relating together, we know each other's inner thoughts and secrets. My husband might say this means he can't get away with anything. But what has happened is that through constant communication, our relationship remains in-sync.

Again, the same principle applies to our relationship with God. Absence from God does not cause the heart to grow fonder as the saying suggests of relationships. In truth, I would argue from personal experience that no relationship grows fonder under absence.

That's a debate I will leave to the experts, but I can speak with some authority from reading God's Word and hearing the voice of Jesus that distance from God can cause an anxious heart. Conversely, when we seek first the kingdom of God—i.e., put God first, love Him above all else, and choose to spend time in His presence—we don't have to be anxious for anything, as Jesus makes clear in His well-known Sermon on the Mount.

> Therefore I tell you, do not worry about your life, what you will eat or drink; or about your body, what you will wear. Is

not life more than food, and the body more than clothes? Look at the birds of the air; they do not sow or reap or store away in barns, and yet your heavenly Father feeds them. Are you not much more valuable than they? Can any one of you by worrying add a single hour to your life? . . . But seek first his kingdom and his righteousness, and all these things will be given to you as well. (Matthew 6:25-34)

Abiding in the presence of our Lord offers us His security. Jesus becomes our shelter, our source of strength, safety, hope, protection, coverage, and assurance (see Psalm 91). Walking and talking with God in the cool of our day is part of our Garden of Eden heritage. That means daily communion with God is part of our make-up. This needs to be our everyday experience if we want to become more in-tune with hearing our Shepherd's voice.

You see, we were created for a permanent relationship with God, not a one-off, breeze-in-breeze-out type of relationship. We can sometimes get caught up in life's busyness as Martha and Mary's story illustrates perfectly. But we were created with intimacy in mind where the Lord shares His secret mysteries with us. We are designed for God's pleasure, and to dwell in His presence is where we belong. Even in everyday menial situations, abiding in Him is the better choice. It is the Mary option.

So many times, I've acted like Martha instead of the better option, Mary. In my early Christian walk, I actually related to Martha far more than to Mary. If I'm honest, I still struggle with a bit of a Martha complex.

In fact, I used to consider Martha somewhat hard-done-by. After all, she was the one trying to bless Jesus with her hospitality. How could that be so wrong? Surely there would be time to sit with the Lord after the chores were done. I mean, it's not being very hospitable to let your guest go hungry, right?

Clearly wrong!

Jesus wants us to feed off Him, the Bread of Life (John 6:35). He wants us to choose Him first and foremost. He longs to impart His truths to us. So many Scriptures contradict our normal way of doing life. Take the passage where Jesus said, "Follow me, and let the dead bury their own dead" (Matthew 8:22). This seems so harsh, almost uncalled for!

But Jesus is saying here, "Put Me first above all else. Leave what you are doing, no matter how important you think it might be, and come abide by My side. Martha (Nicole!), stop busying yourself with menial tasks. Come sit at My feet as Mary did. Let Me impart the revelation-secrets of My promises. I am the better choice."

Jesus made a similar seemingly calloused statement when His mother Mary and brothers came to talk with Him.

> While Jesus was still talking to the crowd, his mother and brothers stood outside, wanting to speak to him. Someone told him, "Your mother and brothers are standing outside, wanting to speak to you". He replied to him, "Who is my mother, and who are my brothers?" Pointing to his disciples, he said, "Here are my mother and my brothers. For whoever does the will of my Father in heaven is my brother and sister and mother. (Matthew 12:46-50)

Did you notice the words standing outside? Jesus's family wasn't leaning in close at that moment. They weren't feeding off every word their Rabbi was teaching. They were outside the inner circle. In this example, Jesus's family was behaving like Martha.

In contrast, His disciples were gathered close to their Shepherd's side. They didn't want to miss a word of the secrets that Jesus had to reveal. Like Mary of Bethany, they made the better choice. They knew where they belonged.

The song lyrics on belonging at the beginning of this section reflected my heart's cry one day in early 2018 and remain my sincere desire even now. As I sat an entire day on the foreshore of a nearby harbour town, I had a desperate longing to hear from God. To have Him speak to me. To have Him teach me how to pray more effectively. To have Him show me the plans He has for me.

As I remained by His side all that day, pressing in, listening to His voice, savouring my Lord's words, I wrote out the lyrics for 'It's Where I Belong'. At that moment, I knew that at His feet was exactly where I needed to be.

Abiding in God's presence is where we hear the voice of our Shepherd. It's where we will be situated to wait for His further instruction. It is out of abiding that we can then be ready to receive and act on Jesus's command. Abiding is the first of our Mary postures, and it is indeed exactly where we belong.

MARY POSTURE

Abide

LESSON # 1: Created in the image of God, we have each been designed for an intimate relationship with our Creator. It's who we are, and by His side is in fact where we belong. Will you choose the Mary posture of abiding? Will you choose to sit at the feet of Jesus so He can reveal His revelation-secrets to you? Will you be Mary rather than Martha today?

Present in His Presence

You will show me the path of life; in your presence is fullness of joy.
—Psalm 16:11 AMP

DEVOTION OF MY HEART

The Essence of Being in His Presence

I love that the word presence is made up largely of another word—essence. Essence is a word that describes being the core of something, the spirit or lifeblood of a particular thing. This essence is a concentrated extract. It is rich, full, and completely undiluted. It is also in its purest form.

To me, this describes beautifully being in the presence of God. God's essence, His Spirit and lifeblood, perfectly and richly saturates us, pours out over us and into us in absolute abundance. This essence is the sweet, aromatic perfume of His love. The glorious infusion of His life-giving blood. The centrality of the gift of grace He has offered us.

All of this is the true essence of being in God's presence. And we in turn as vessels of His Spirit carry His essence everywhere we go.

In a large house there are articles not only of gold and silver but also of wood and clay; some are for special purposes and some for common use. Those who cleanse themselves from the latter will be instruments for special purposes, made holy, useful to the Master, and prepared to do any good work. (2 Timothy 2:20-21)

CHAPTER FOUR

The Present

God, your wrap-around presence is our defense. In your kindness look upon the faces of your anointed ones. For just one day of intimacy with you is like a thousand days of joy rolled into one.

— Psalm 84:9-10 TPT

When it comes to my children's early childhood years, I can now admit their birthday parties have been regrettably marked by perfectionism. I was definitely more Martha than Mary when it came to a themed party. I wanted my children to have the perfect party, but this was more for my needs than theirs. Instead of just enjoying their special day, I used all my time and energy trying to create a perfect day for them. There is a big difference! In the process, I not only exhausted myself but spent a fortune.

My children couldn't have cared less if the napkins matched the table runner or if the balloons were colour-coordinated metallic and helium-filled rather than a mishmash of supermarket latex balloons. Unfortunately, I *could* care less. Which was how an otherwise perfectly matched pink and white polka-dot themed fourth birthday party for Faith turned into an idealistic mother's meltdown when an hour before the party all those specially purchased, helium-filled balloons began to pop. Leaving Faith's perfectionist mum with no choice but to quickly organise the purchase of some multi-coloured supermarket brands.

Of course, my children weren't even old enough to know the difference. As I look back, I now recognise that a balloon is a balloon. In fact, for a four-year-old's birthday party, the more colourful the balloons the more enticing they undoubtedly were.

My children just wanted a fun, present mum, not a crazy, everything-has-to-be-perfect mum. They wanted Mary, not Martha. My present to them should have been to be *present* in their presence. Or as my middle son Joel often quotes out of the *Kung Fu Panda* movie, an expression originally coined by the longest-standing first lady of the United States, Eleanor Roosevelt:

> Yesterday is history, tomorrow is a mystery and today is a gift. That is why it is called the present.

My presence alone would have been present enough for my children's birthday parties. It would have brought

The Present

them the fullness of joy (Psalm 16:11).

I have since learned from my early motherhood party-planning obsession. I still love creating beautiful spaces for birthdays, Christmas, dinner parties, and other events. In fact, staging is one of my favourite pastimes. But I've learned to do it from a place of rest rather than works.

Just as my party-planning perfectionism took me away from simply being present with my children, I've come to see that the same perfectionism can keep us from being present in God's presence. In this next section, we will continue examining our first Mary posture of *abiding*. But this time, I want to address those areas in our lives that may be holding us back from coming into our Father's presence in the first place.

We will also look together at the redeeming love gifted to us through Christ's blood sacrifice that makes us worthy and whole, presenting us perfect to our heavenly Father without any merit of our own. If we are to experience intimate communion with God even when our shortcomings want to hinder us from coming into His presence, we have to fully receive the redeeming love He has for us, which is the grace gift we have been given.

Unlike perfectionism, which requires striving for something that is actually unattainable, our heavenly Father doesn't ask anything from us when it comes to a relationship with Him. In fact, when our lives are hidden with Christ in God (Colossians 3:3), Jesus has us covered. His perfection becomes our perfection. In Him, we become the righteousness of God.

> God made him who had no sin to be sin for us, so that in him we might become the righteousness of God.
> (2 Corinthians 5:21)

In other words, when we choose Jesus as our Saviour, our heavenly Father sees us through the 'lens' of His unblemished Son Jesus, perfect and whole. We can come into God's presence just as we are even in all our messiness.

This is an amazing present we have been given, yet many of us struggle to accept this truth. Certainly my own feelings of unworthiness have at times hindered me over the years from coming into my Father's presence. I have struggled to choose the better Mary option of *abiding* in God's presence despite my failings, retreating from God rather than drawing closer as He invites.

In this battle with perfectionism, I've also found myself trying to *earn* God's favour rather than accept that my worth comes only through Jesus. Thankfully, I've come to see over time that becoming worthy in God's eyes through my own efforts is unachievable. In fact Isaiah 64:6 tells us that all our best efforts are but filthy rags before the Lord.

In other words, striving to please God or earn God's favour is exhausting and ultimately cancels out Christ's amazing gift of unmerited favour. Because as most of us know, a present cannot be earned. That is why it is called a gift in the first place. And the gift we have been given was bought at the highest cost as the epistle to the Hebrews reminds us.

The Present

> Our High Priest [Jesus] offered himself to God as a single sacrifice for sins, good for all time . . . For by that one offering he forever made perfect those who are being made holy. (Hebrews 10:12,14 NLT)

Through our union with Jesus, we are constantly being transformed more and more into His likeness (2 Corinthians 3:18). This is great news. But this is an ongoing transformation. We will never be perfect this side of heaven. Only Christ is perfect. It is Jesus, the righteous One, who makes us right with God. It is through Christ's sacrifice only that we have been given full, uninhibited entrance to abide in our Father's house as the writer of the epistle to the Hebrews also highlights.

> And now we are brothers and sisters in God's family because of the blood of Jesus, and he welcomes us to come into the most holy sanctuary in the heavenly realm – boldly and without hesitation. For he has dedicated a new, life-giving way for us to approach God. For just as the veil was torn in two, Jesus' body was torn open to give us free and fresh access to him. And since we now have a magnificent High Priest to welcome us into God's house, we come closer to God and approach him with an open heart, fully convinced that nothing will keep us at a distance from him. For our hearts have been sprinkled with blood to remove impurity, and we have been freed from an accusing conscience. Now we are clean, unstained, and presentable to God inside and out. (Hebrews 10:19-22 TPT)

Jesus has paved the way for us to enjoy true intimate union with our heavenly Father. Our Garden of Eden heritage of perpetual abiding in God's presence has been gifted to us through Jesus. Because of His atoning sacrifice, our Father now welcomes us into the most holy sanctuary in the heavenly realm with nothing inhibiting that union. In fact, God desires communion with us so much that He stands at the door of our hearts, knocking and waiting eagerly for us to invite Him in (Revelation 3:20).

This means that God is not looking for perfection from us before we can commune with Him. As the well-known twentieth-century American evangelist Kathryn Kuhlman once expressed it, God is not looking for gold vessels or silver vessels, but for 'willing vessels'. Or as Jesus put it, "worshippers who desire to worship the Father in spirit and in truth" (John 4:23-24, author's paraphrase).

This is the good news message of Jesus Christ. Yet many of us still struggle to fully comprehend such an amazing gift that has been bestowed upon us. Like me, you may toggle from time to time with feelings of unworthiness, guilt, shame, or some other emotion that hinders our being present in our Father's presence when we feel less than holy. Some may even run away and hide from God as Adam and Eve did when guilt first entered their existence after they disobeyed God by eating from the tree of the knowledge of good and evil.

The Present

> When the woman saw that the fruit of the tree was good for food and pleasing to the eye, and also desirable for gaining wisdom, she took some and ate it. She also gave some to her husband, who was with her, and he ate it. Then the eyes of both of them were opened, and they realized they were naked; so they sewed fig leaves together and made coverings for themselves. Then the man and his wife heard the sound of the Lord God as he was walking in the garden in the cool of the day, and they hid from the Lord God among the trees of the garden. (Genesis 3:6-8)

Adam and Eve became aware of their sinful nature the moment they ate from the forbidden fruit. Shame and guilt then clothed their once perfectly content naked bodies, so they immediately tried to cover up and hide from God's gaze as He walked throughout the garden. Something many of us still try to do to this day.

Certainly when I've conversed with God on this subject, I've seen areas in my own life that inhibit my feeling worthy enough to abide in His presence. A feeling not shared by my Lord since it is not by my own righteousness that I enter His holy sanctuary in the first place but only through Jesus's righteousness.

The reality is, we all sin. This is the inevitable fall of mankind since the beginning of time. We all fall short of the glory of God (Romans 3:23), as the apostle Paul reminds us, and there will always be a tug-of-war that rages between our flesh man and our spirit man (Romans 7:22-23). That is why we need a mediator in Jesus, as Paul also recognised.

> So who has the power to rescue this miserable man from the unwelcome intruder of sin and death? I give all my thanks to God, for his mighty power has finally proved a way out through our Lord Jesus, the Anointed One! (Romans 7:24-25 TPT)

In their shame, Adam and Eve hid themselves from God's presence because they expected that God would not want to commune with them in that unworthy state. Something to which I can well relate. And yet Adam and Eve misread the depth of their heavenly Father's love, something we may be doing as well. Because instead of shunning Adam and Eve when they went undercover after their disobedient actions, God came looking for them (Genesis 3:9). It is always God who comes in pursuit of His children. It's His very nature to leave the ninety-nine and go after the one lost sheep (Luke 15:4). It is God's way to welcome home the squandering, reckless prodigal son or daughter and crown them in a royal robe (Luke 15:13-24). God never gives up on His beloved.

His children's separation from God has always provoked an emotional outcry from our beautiful Father. We see His merciful ways and redemptive love all the way throughout biblical history. The testimony of Hosea and Gomer, which we will look at later, especially reveals that there is no story God can't redeem.

Adam and Eve's sin resulted in God removing them from the Garden of Eden. Even their banishment was still an act of God's mercy so that they would not eat from the tree of life and live eternally in their sins (Genesis 3:21-

24). But that story of separation and banishment need no longer be our story because God sent His Son Jesus to become the sacrificial lamb so that through His death and resurrection all the lost sheep of the world could be brought back into an intimate relationship with the Father.

In other words, Jesus became the new *symbolic* Garden of Eden. This means we can walk tall in His righteousness. We no longer have to walk in shame and guilt. Nor do we need to run away, cover-up, or hide from the presence of the Lord when we do not feel worthy because Jesus has us covered. He is the *present* that enables us to be in our Father's *presence*.

We do not have to earn this precious gift. In fact, there is nothing we can ever do to deserve it. Christ 'deserved' it on our behalf. God's rich mercy has made us alive with Christ, and we are perfectly imperfect because of Jesus's perfect sacrifice.

CHAPTER FIVE

Perfectly Imperfect

By [Jesus's] one perfect sacrifice he made us perfectly holy and complete for all time.

—Hebrews 10:14 TPT

Over the years, I have had numerous conversations with Jesus on the subject of His redeeming grace. Mostly because I have struggled with perfectionism, as you just saw in the previous chapter. So redemption sometimes seems too good to be true. I haven't always felt worthy or perfect enough to receive such an unmerited gift. This is, of course, the point of the gift of grace. It cannot be earned.

But there were two distinct occasions in my life when Jesus explained His redemption to me in greater clarity. The first visual aid I received was through the ocean's waves. The second was through the cleansing properties of snow. Both the ocean and snow are made up overwhelmingly of water. Through these visuals, Jesus revealed to me the similarities of His blood, which makes us pure and clean and which is also made up predominantly of water.

One way I have pictured our sins being completely washed clean is like when our stain-covered clothing is put through the cleansing cycles of our washing machines as King David described in one of his psalms.

> Soak me in your laundry and I'll come out clean, scrub me and I'll have a snow-white life. (Psalm 51:7 MSG)

We too as God's children are being perpetually washed clean by the blood of the Lamb, cycle after cycle. So what our heavenly Father sees is not our former sinful nature but our newly-washed, snowy-clean Christ-likeness. This is Jesus's redeeming grace.

The washing machine is a good analogy of the redemption we have in Christ. But it was during a family vacation on a Gold Coast beach in Australia's northern state of Queensland that Jesus first spoke to me on this subject of His redeeming blood, revealing pictorially through the ocean's waves how our sins are being constantly washed away and fully forgotten.

Walking along the shoreline in the glow of one of our perfect South Pacific sunrises, I noted how every few steps a new wave would come along, washing away the prints of my feet indented into well-soaked sand and leaving no trace I'd ever walked there. This, I realised, is what our sins look like to our Father when we abide inside of Christ. We will continue to sin throughout our days on this earth, the inevitable result of mankind's fall.

But through our union with the Son of God, through Christ's forgiveness and perfect righteousness, and ultimately because of the finished work of the cross, all our sins are washed away. They will never surface again as the waves washing away my footprints showed me and numerous Scriptures remind us.

> I, even I, am he who blots out your transgressions, for my own sake, and remembers your sins no more. (Isaiah 43:25)

> For I will forgive their wickedness and will remember their sins no more. (Hebrews 8:12)

> Who is a God like you, who pardons sin and forgives the transgression . . . You will again have compassion on us; you will tread our sins underfoot and hurl all our iniquities into the depths of the sea. (Micah 7:18-19)

The millions of footprints that have marked the shores of our planet's beaches throughout history can never resurface because the ocean washes them clean away, wave after wave. This is the same cleansing process of God's mercy towards us as Mary, the mother of Jesus, recognised when she sang the good news (Magnificat) that she was to bear the Messiah.

His mercy flows in wave after wave on those who are in awe before him. (Luke 1:50 MSG)

Another illustration I was given of the cleansing gift of the blood of Jesus occurred during my twentieth wedding anniversary. Jamie and I had ventured for a long weekend away to one of Australia's most pristine islands off the most southerly part of our country, Tasmania. We travelled in August, which was toward the tail end of our Australian winter. Jamie and I made our way straight to a World Heritage-listed wilderness area known as Cradle Mountain in the central highlands of the Lake St Clair National Park district. We had our hearts set on hiking around the mountain as well as walking the perimeters of the spectacular Lake St Clair.

There was only one problem. We had just arrived in Cradle Mountain when an unprecedented snowstorm set in, closing down the entire region. The mountain was deemed highly dangerous to climb and therefore out of bounds for hikers. The lake was closed off for similar reasons. All our plans went out the window.

Well, almost. How should I put this nicely? The reality is that my husband has a bit of a rebellious streak. Admittedly, what came next wasn't his intention. Nevertheless, the defiant side of his nature enjoyed our misadventure enormously.

Our day had started with what we'd thought would be a simple stroll around a thirty-minute loop still open to the public at the base of the mountain that was known as the Enchanted Walk. We'd taken only a small bottle of

Perfectly Imperfect

water with us as we expected to be back at the hotel in no time at all. I'd worn a favourite pair of fashion boots purchased in Paris earlier that year, so I was definitely not prepared for how our day actually unfolded.

Jamie and I were thoroughly enjoying what we thought would be a brief meander through this magical rainforest and cascading river. In fact, the newly fallen snow made the forest even more mystical than usual. And so we lost ourselves in exploration—literally!

It was well into our supposedly easy thirty-minute stroll when we realised we'd not only ventured away from the forest floor and were now heading up the mountain but that we hadn't seen a direction sign for some time. Nor had we seen any other hikers on this supposed all-abilities track. We were without water, with non-grip shoes, in icy conditions, and with only the sun to hopefully guide us. Still, Jamie and I chose to keep climbing up Cradle Mountain rather than retrace our steps back.

At times our trek got a little harrowing. There were some steep sections where I needed Jamie's strength to get me up. There were also some very icy, narrow-edged ledges that were not conducive to non-grip shoes. By the third hour of our arduous trek, we even had a rescue helicopter circling over us regularly. This was one misadventure we would never forget.

So what is the point to my story, and how does the blood of Jesus fit into our twentieth wedding anniversary escapade? Through our boots, oddly enough. You see, both Jamie's more rugged work boots and my fashionable Paris ankle-boots became completely scuffed and filthy with mud during our climb. At one point, I even complained to Jamie that I'd ruined a favourite pair of footwear and that neither sets of boots would be salvageable after this ordeal.

Then we hiked through an acre's worth of knee-high snow. For me, this was the hardest part of our ordeal as my legs were exhausted and I kept face-planting into a mountain of snow every other step. We finally made it back to our hotel room, completely exhausted, dehydrated, cold, and wet-through. We tugged off our boots and set them by the heater, after which we collapsed into bed and slept for a solid couple of hours.

We awoke to something quite bizarre. Both Jamie's rugged work boots and my fashion boots had been washed clean by the snow. Dried through by the heater, these boots we'd thought to be unsalvageable were now the cleanest boots either of us had ever owned. In fact, they looked as if they'd been made brand-new. In the Old Testament book of Isaiah, God describes our sins in a similar 'impossible' fashion.

> "Come now, let us settle the matter," says the Lord. "Though your sins are like scarlet they shall be as white as snow; though they are red as crimson, they shall be like wool." (Isaiah 1:18)

The ocean waves that washed away my footprints and our little misadventure that led to our boots being cleansed by crystal-white snow are both beautiful reminders to me that Jesus washes away our sins and makes us a brand new creation in and through our abiding in Him. The apostle Paul affirms this truth.

> Therefore, if anyone is in Christ, the new creation has come: The old has gone, the new is here! (2 Corinthians 5:17)

We are perfectly imperfect in Christ because we are a brand-new creation inside of Jesus's perfection and the Father sees us clean and perfectly whole through His beloved Son. Jesus is the One who washes away our sins and makes us white as snow, and we are perpetually cleansed by the redeeming blood of the Lamb.

This is something to which the second Mary I want to introduce could very likely testify after her own encounter with Jesus. This Mary was born in a town called Magdala, so she is referenced in the Gospel accounts as 'the Magdalene' or just Mary Magdalene, i.e., someone from that town. A significant figure in Jesus's ministry, Mary Magdalene is mentioned numerous times in the Gospels. Many of these references are together with Mary the mother of Jesus and other women such as Joanna and Susanna, who faithfully served and financially supported Jesus and His missional work.

Mary Magdalene became a devoted follower of Jesus and is often depicted abiding close to her Rabbi. In fact, she was the first person to see the resurrected Christ. But she was a very different person before she met Jesus. She was actually known in her region for being afflicted with seven demonic influences (Luke 8:2).

Everything changed for Mary Magdalene when she had an encounter with Jesus. She was liberated from these horrible demonic afflictions, released from the grip of the evil one, washed completely clean, and made into a brand new creation. From that one encounter with Jesus, Mary's life completely turned around.

In *The Chosen*, a film series on Jesus's ministry, Mary Magdalene is trying to explain her healing to Nicodemus, a Pharisee and member of the Sanhedrin, when she makes the following powerful statement: "I was one way, and now I am completely different. And the thing that happened in between . . . was Him!"

Jesus makes all things new. Once she met Jesus, Mary Magdalene became a brand-new creation, 'one way' before Jesus and now 'completely different' in Him. Likewise, our own 'crucifixion with Christ has severed the tie to this life, and now [our] true life is hidden away in God in Christ' (Colossians 3:3 TPT).

In other words, through Jesus we have been purchased, bought back, and saved by His amazing grace. We are perfectly imperfect inside of His perfection. We are wrapped up completely by the redeeming love of our Saviour God. As we will see highlighted through Hosea and Gomer's story next, this means there really is no story God can't redeem.

CHAPTER SIX

No Story God Can't Redeem

You are my dear children, and I write these things to you so that you won't sin. But if anyone does sin, we continually have a forgiving Redeemer who is face-to-face with the Father; Jesus Christ, the Righteous One. He is the atoning sacrifice for our sins, and not only for ours but also for the sins of the whole world.

—1 John 2:1-2 TPT

While God had been working in me on the topic of grace, I still wrestled with letting go of unworthiness, shame, and guilt. I wanted to understand in more depth how these feelings might prevent me from abiding in God's presence, let alone stepping into the other two Mary postures of *waiting* and *receiving*. And so the Spirit of God led me to the word *redeemed*.

According to my Google search engine, redeemed is a word that means to be re-purchased, re-possessed, bought back, and saved. These are words that describe us as having always been God's. We are His most beloved, and when we accept Jesus as our Lord and Saviour, He simply reclaims that which belonged to Him in the first place—us!

At this same time, God also showed me that He is our number one fan. He is championing us on. When we fall, He doesn't growl at us. He isn't there rolling His eyes, pointing His finger, and trying to come up with a good form of punishment.

Instead, He picks us up, swings us in His arms, lovingly sets us back down, on the right path this time, and encourages us to give life another go. The next time we fall—and we will!—He does it all over again. God is our greatest champion. He is the most loving Father of all.

While this was a good reminder, I wasn't fully satisfied on this occasion with my heavenly Papa's response. I wanted to see another perspective of how God's grace abounds in the lives of all. So on one of my morning walks and talks, God showed me a number of biblical characters who had each made multiple mistakes, all had their own list of flawed character traits, and yet still received God's redeeming love and unmerited favour.

These range from Mary Magdalene, oppressed by seven demons prior to her encounter with Jesus (Luke

8:2), to the prophet Jonah, who blatantly rebelled against God's call to deliver a prophetic message to the city of Nineveh (Jonah 1). Even Moses, destined for a great leadership role, had a moment of rage that saw him killing an Egyptian guard, then fleeing into the wilderness, where he hid from his true calling for forty-years (Exodus 2).

Then there was the Samaritan woman who met Jesus while drawing water from Jacob's well. She'd already had five husbands and was living out-of-wedlock with a man at the time she encountered the Messiah (John 4:18). King David was called a man after God's own heart (1 Samuel 13:14), yet he had an adulterous affair with Bathsheba then went on to murder her husband (2 Samuel 11). The apostle Paul was also someone with a disreputable past. Then known as Saul, he was a leading persecutor of the early church, infamous for his murderous attacks against followers of Jesus (Acts 9:1-2).

These and other men and women we now know as mighty warriors of the faith were pursued by God despite their human failings and went on to receive His favour and promotion. Mary Magdalene became a devout follower of Jesus, always abiding close by His side (Mark 15:40-41). Jonah was given a second chance to prophesy the word of the Lord to the city of Nineveh, destined for destruction. This time Jonah obeyed God and the people of Nineveh were saved (Jonah 3). Moses emerged from the wilderness to take up his calling as leader of the Israelite nation. In the process, he became a personal friend of God's, communing with God regularly face-to-face (Exodus 33:11).

The Samaritan woman at Jacob's well also received promotion. After receiving the truth that Jesus is the Messiah, this woman received her destiny as the first ever New Testament evangelist. Many from her Samaritan village believed in Jesus because of her testimony (John 4:39). Restored back into right relationship with God, David became the greatest king Israel ever knew (2 Samuel 8:14). As for Paul, he went from being persecutor to an apostle and forefather of the Christian faith while his New Testament epistles have influenced Christendom ever since, including on the topic of God's redeeming grace (1 Corinthians 15:9-10).

In all these scenarios, God pursued His people and redeemed their lives according to the riches of His graces. All of their flaws, faults, shortcomings, and mistakes did not prevent God from going after them because His unmerited grace is for everyone.

Our loving Father is championing us all on for greater things to come. These men and women of the faith are not the exceptions but our examples. God's mercy is unending, and His grace continues to super-abound in our lives, something the Father revealed to me in greater depth through the redeeming love story of Hosea and his wife Gomer.

To me, Hosea and Gomer's story is the perfect illustration of God's redeeming love for all of mankind. It foreshadows the ultimate redemptive story found in the sacrifice of Jesus. It also shows us that our mess can indeed become a message of hope.

This certainly proved true for Hosea as he endured

a messy relationship with his adulterous wife Gomer. God used that mess as a message of redemption for the entire Israelite nation. You see, God handpicked Gomer to be Hosea's wife. Some scholars believe Gomer was a temple prostitute, a common practice in Baal worship, when Hosea married her. Others suggest she simply had a licentious lifestyle. Either way, she was chosen by God to be Hosea's bride.

> Go marry a promiscuous woman and have children with her, for like an adulterous wife this land is guilty of unfaithfulness to the Lord. (Hosea 1:2)

This seems like the most bizarre bridal choice for a man like Hosea who was walking in close obedience with God. But I think that is actually the point to this story. God chose His servant Hosea for this important assignment because He needed someone He could trust to rescue His daughter, Gomer. After all, God will always pursue the one lost sheep and will go to extraordinary lengths to redeem even one.

God also needed someone to deliver the same message of repentance and deliverance to His own bride, Israel, who was mirroring Gomer's unfaithful behaviour, prostituting themselves to other gods (Hosea 4:12). Because of Hosea's faithful obedience, God chose to partner with Hosea to deliver His gift of grace to Gomer and the nation of Israel.

Gomer and Israel were both reciprocates of God's unmerited favour and His redeeming love. Neither deserved God's attention, let alone His redemption. Gomer was known as a promiscuous woman when Hosea married her. After bearing three children, she broke her marital covenant and returned to a life of promiscuity, first as an adulteress, then an actual sex slave until Hosea bought her out of slavery (Hosea 3:1-3).

Israel had also been redeemed from slavery in the most miraculous fashion (Exodus 14). But they turned their back on the God who had rescued them, idolising other gods. Yet God still pursued them over and again. I love that Hosea's name means salvation. It was such a prophetically appointed name as he went on to be a type of scapegoat in this story.

In Mosaic law, the scapegoat was burdened with all the sins of the Israelites, leaving the people ritually cleansed of their sins (Leviticus 16). Over time, the term scapegoat came to mean any innocent person or group that bears the sins or blame of others. This was another foreshadowing of the ultimate scapegoat, Jesus Christ, who though unblemished and without sin became sin through His blood sacrifice in order to offer eternal salvation to the entire world (2 Corinthians 5:21).

Like Jesus, Hosea didn't deserve to be the scapegoat in this scenario. He was walking closely to God, a man of reputable character. It cost Hosea a great sum of money and most likely his dignity when God instructed him to redeem his wife out of the slave-like adulterous lifestyle she found herself in (Hosea 3:1-5).

To make matters worse, his personal mess was to become public knowledge when God told him to prophesy a similar message of repentance to the Israelite nation, urging them to turn from prostituting themselves to other gods and return instead back to the one true living God (Hosea 14:4). In summary, Hosea became the necessary scapegoat to proclaim a message of redemption for all of God's beloved.

God will often use our past hurts, mistakes, and mess to deliver a message of His redeeming love. This was certainly Hosea's story, and it's been my experience as well. Through a nine-year faith journey to have children, my testing most definitely became a testimony of God's mercy, grace, steadfast love, and faithfulness (Exodus 34:6). From personal and matrimonial healing to spiritual rebuilding, God wrought restoration, victory, and freedom in all of these areas in my life. I am living proof that there really is no story God can't redeem and that our mess can indeed become a message of hope.

Sometimes God will pursue us in the most outlandish of ways. Jonah was pursued right into a giant fish's belly so that God could realign his destiny (Jonah 1:17). God gained Moses's attention by speaking through a non-extinguishing burning bush (Exodus 3). The Samaritan woman at Jacob's well was spoken to directly by the Son of God. Through this one encounter, she not only received salvation but through her testimony a whole village of Samaritans were redeemed (John 4:1-42).

Along the road to Damascus, Jesus blinded Saul's eyes to redirect Saul's brutal aggression towards Jesus's followers and give him brand new Christ-centred vision (Acts 9:1-19). It was through a word of knowledge from the prophet Nathan that King David recognised and repented from his lustful ways (2 Samuel 12). It was through the prophet Hosea that both Gomer and Israel were redeemed back to the Father (Hosea 3:1-4, Hosea 14).

In all of these circumstances, God showed His great mercy and compassion, radically pursuing where necessary. God wants to restore all of His beloved back into right standing with Him. He wants to reclaim that which belongs to Him in the first place—us. My own redemptive love story that came through a desperate desire to become a mum is living proof that God restores to this very day.

In Gomer's example, Hosea needed to lay down his own desires in order to save her life. He had to trust and obey God implicitly throughout the redemptive process, and he ultimately had to offer grace and forgiveness to someone who many would have considered an unworthy reciprocate of such unmerited favour.

This is God's story for all of mankind as well. Not one of us deserves His grace. And yet we can receive it freely because God loves the world so much that He sent His only begotten Son Jesus to lay down His life in order to restore, reconcile, and redeem us back into right standing with our heavenly Father (John 3:16). Just how far is God willing to pursue you? All the way to a painful death in your place on a cross. Because there really is no story God can't redeem. He just wants us to accept His amazing gift of grace and enjoy being present in His presence.

MARY POSTURE

Abide

LESSON # 2: To be present in God's presence is the greatest present we can ever receive. It is the fullness of joy. Will you choose to come into the presence of God just as you are, perfectly imperfect because of Jesus's perfection? Will you accept the redeeming grace of God that shows us there really is no story God can't redeem? Will you choose the Mary posture of abiding today? Because He just wants you!

Queen In Waiting

And who knows but that you have come to your royal position for such a time as this?
—Esther 4:14

DEVOTION OF MY HEART

An Audience with the King

An audience with the king was all it took for a young Jewish orphan girl named Esther to change the future for her marginalised people. Esther was born for such a time as to save her people from annihilation. Her selection as queen of Persia and her subsequent audience with King Xerxes, risking her own life to plead for the lives of her people, changed Esther's personal destiny as well as all of Jewish history.

An audience with our King changes our history too. We were born for such a time as this!

CHAPTER SEVEN

Season Of Waiting

> Let this hope burst forth within you, releasing a continual joy. Don't give up in a time of trouble, but commune with God at all times.
>
> — Romans 12:12 TPT

On one of my early morning walks, I asked for a Scripture from God specific to my current circumstances. I didn't want a well-known verse but something I wouldn't typically think of so that it *felt* more legitimately given to me by God's Spirit. That may sound self-indulgent as though I was acting like a spoilt child dictating what sort of word I might receive from God. But my heart's desire was pure enough.

You see, I had a yearning to know the plans God has for me, a pattern you will notice in my life's journey. I desperately wanted to know I was on the right course and not just floundering, off-track, or even lost. So I asked to receive as Jesus Himself invites us to do.

> I tell you: ask, and you shall receive; seek, and you shall find; knock, and the door shall be opened to you. For everyone who asks, receives; and everyone who seeks, finds; and to everyone who knocks the door will be opened.
> (Luke 11:9-10)

The Scripture God ended up giving me on this particular day turned out not to be so ambiguous or unfamiliar. In fact, it is a passage that speakers at almost every Christian women's conference I've ever attended have offered as a source of encouragement to the womenfolk in their audience. The words are actually those of Esther's adoptive father, Mordecai, when he calls for her to risk her own life by approaching the king uninvited to petition for her people.

> And who knows but that you have come to your royal position for such a time as this. (Esther 4:14)

God does have a sense of humour! That said, while I've long known the basics of Esther's story, the book of Esther certainly hasn't been a go-to book of the Bible for me. I hadn't pondered much on that particular Scripture nor had I considered Esther's story as applicable to my own spiritual walk. But on this particular morning, the above verse and in fact the entire book of Esther provoked much thought and conversation with my Papa.

You see, I'd been waiting for a specific answer

to prayer. Some months earlier, I had forwarded the manuscript of my first book *Having Faith* to a publishing house in the UK, and I was eagerly waiting to hear back. I had put all my eggs in this one basket, this one publishing house, as I'd felt that God had given me an image of a lion as a symbol that my book would be published through a company with the word lion in its name. Every day for about a year, I'd seen a lion in some shape or form that seemed to confirm what I sensed God had shown me.

Now it may sound far-fetched that I saw a lion every day, especially living in Australia where the only lions we have are found in the zoo. But for those of you who have read my first book, you will know that sometimes God shows me pictures as a confirmation that I am on the right track. In *Having Faith*, I write about seeing rainbows every day for an entire month as a promised sign that my nine-year faith journey was coming to an end. I also mention a whale that God used to confirm His intent for me to remain in an assignment I was uncomfortable leading.

In more recent times, God has used eagles to show me His providence while I journey another queen-in-waiting season. I'll leave that story for another book, but it has certainly been the case that God chooses at times to communicate to me in this way. It is further illustration of God's unconventional communication methods, as I mentioned at the beginning of this book.

On this occasion, God used lions throughout an entire year to keep me on track for my God-appointed destiny. The London Christian publisher to which I'd forwarded my book fit this imagery perfectly. So with a lion around every corner, I waited for almost a year with a conviction that I would hear back from them favourably.

In time, God revealed to me that this wasn't the path He'd chosen for my book after all. But on that day several months earlier when I received the Esther Scripture, I sensed God showing me that I was in a time of waiting, a time of preparation. I had not yet come into the fullness of my calling. I was what I came to term a 'queen-in-waiting'.

Not so dissimilar to Esther, who needed a year of purification and cleansing before she could have an audience with the king (Esther 2:12), God wants to refine each of us too, and during this waiting period for a publishing deal, I found myself being prepared just as Esther had been during her time as queen-in-waiting.

We see other faithful followers of God in the Bible experiencing something similar prior to their destiny being fulfilled. Before the Israelites could enter the Promised Land, they were instructed to set up a monument of stones at the edge of the Jordan River so they would never forget that God had brought them out of slavery (Joshua 4). They then needed to sanctify themselves through the purification act of circumcision before God gave them their first victory at the city of Jericho (Joshua 5). For the Israelites, this involved a letting go of their past in order for them to step into their new Promised Land.

David also went through a season of refinement. He was appointed the next king of Israel, but he spent many long years living in the wilderness and hiding in caves before the time came to step into his God-appointed destiny (1 Samuel 21-23). It was in these fearful, challenging times that David learned to trust God and praise Him above all else (Psalm 56).

Moses spent forty years in the wilderness before being appointed by God as leader of the Israelite nation (Acts 7:30). After his Damascus road enlightenment, the apostle Paul spent a three-year 'wilderness' training period with Jesus Himself before beginning his missionary career (Galatians 1:11-20).

Even Jesus's own ministry had an appointed time. Only after His water baptism where the Holy Spirit rested upon His shoulders did His ministry really begin (Matthew 3:13-17). And He was first sent into the wilderness where He fasted for forty days and forty nights, after which the devil tried to tempt Him away from His destiny (Matthew 4:1-11).

In other words, God-assignments often require a queen-in-waiting season before God fulfils His promised destiny for our lives and brings to fruition the ministries to which He has called us. This has certainly been my experience. Every time a new ministry has been birthed in my life or an increase in already occurring ministry, it has first required a type of wilderness experience. It is in those wilderness seasons of purification that our Father refines us and that we learn to wait and lean on Him even more.

> This third I will put into the fire; I will refine them like silver and test them like gold. They will call on my name and I will answer them; I will say, "They are my people," and they will say, "The Lord is our God." (Zechariah 13:9)

Throughout that entire year of seeing lions, God was refining the gifts I would need for the next stage of my calling. He was growing my ability to hear His voice more clearly. He was training me to trust His direction implicitly. I was being shown the benefit of positioning myself in stillness to wait (sometimes less than patiently!) for His next set of instructions.

This season of waiting was something Mary Magdalene also experienced. So in this next section, I want to explore a little more of the second Mary posture of *waiting* by looking at Mary Magdalene's example as well as Queen Esther's year in preparation and my own season of biding time in readiness for God's directive for my life.

As we saw in prior chapters, there is much to love about Mary Magdalene and so many principles we can glean from her story. But in terms of posturing ourselves to wait, let's cast our eyes to one of the last glimpses we have of Mary in John 20. Specifically, the scene where Jesus's body has been entombed three days and three nights after He suffered a horrific crucifixion death.

Mary had stayed by Jesus's side throughout His entire deathly ordeal, journeying from Galilee to Jerusalem and continuing to minister to her Lord along with the other women in Jesus's party as He carried the torturous cross to its final resting place and humanity's darkest hour (Mark 15:41). She was among the last present when Jesus drew His final breath (Matthew 27:55-56). She was also one of the women keeping a grieving vigil as Joseph from Arimathea wrapped Jesus's body and placed Him in a new garden tomb (Luke 23:55-56).

Season Of Waiting

Throughout the death and resurrection of Jesus, Mary Magdalene's posture is one of waiting, residing close to her Saviour's side, ministering to Jesus even after His death. So it is little wonder that on the third day as soon as the Sabbath was finished and she could lawfully resume vigilance, Mary again went to wait on her Lord.

> Early on the first day of the week, while it was still dark, Mary Magdalene went to the tomb and saw that the stone had been removed from the entrance. So she came running to Simon Peter and the other disciple, the one Jesus loved, and said, "They have taken the Lord out of the tomb, and we don't know where they have put him!" (John 20:1-2)

I love that Mary was respected and trusted by the disciples so much that when she informed them Jesus was not in the tomb, two disciples, Peter and John known affectionately as 'the one Jesus loved', ran immediately to the tomb to look for Jesus's body themselves. But I also find it interesting that once they'd confirmed Jesus's body was indeed missing, Peter and John didn't position themselves to wait at the tomb as Mary did. Instead they went back to where they were staying (John 20:10).

The point here is that waiting reaps rewards. It enables God to orchestrate whatever is needed behind the scenes that we can't see in the natural world. By posturing herself to wait at the last place she had seen Jesus's body, i.e., at the tomb, Mary positioned herself to receive what no other human can boast to have received.

> Now Mary stood [waiting] outside the tomb crying. As she wept, she bent over to look into the tomb and saw two angels in white, seated where Jesus's body had been, one at the head and the other at the foot. They asked her, "Woman, why are you crying?" "They have taken my Lord away," she said, "and I don't know where they have put him." At this, she turned around and saw Jesus standing there…(John 20:11-14).

In her posture of waiting, Mary received a beautiful gift. Not only was she privy to the angelic beings assigned to minister to Jesus Himself, which on its own would have been extraordinary to witness, but by stationing herself there to wait, Mary was the first to have the resurrected Saviour reveal Himself to her (John 20:14-15). Jesus chose to disclose His true identity as the resurrected King of all kings, God Himself, to the only one who had chosen to wait. And He did it with one tender, loving word that must have melted her heart. "Mary!"

How breath-taking that moment must have been. Oh, to hear your name called by God as Mary did! What an intimate exchange must have taken place. To me, this is one of the most beautiful scenes in the Bible. Mary doesn't actually recognise Jesus until she hears His familiar voice tenderly speaking her name. She is immediately so overcome with emotion that she clings to Him, crying out, "Rabboni," which means teacher in Aramaic (John 20:15-17).

In Mary's time of waiting, she received much. She was rewarded for her faithfulness. By choosing to abide permanently, by Jesus's side, she was elevated and promoted. Because she stood ready to receive her resurrected Master, she was blessed with the spreading of the good news that Jesus was indeed alive, that she'd actually seen and conversed with her Deliverer, that she'd embraced her Saviour God. By waiting for Jesus, Mary was completely honoured in return.

Waiting with eager anticipation as Mary did and as we will see further in the story of Queen Esther reaps amazing results. But as my own story will also testify, waiting is not always easy. Sometimes we must learn to relinquish our own will to that of our heavenly Father in order to receive what He has orchestrated in the first place.

CHAPTER EIGHT

Not My Will But Yours

Don't give up; don't be impatient; be entwined as one with the Lord. Be brave and courageous, and never lose hope. Yes, keep on waiting – for he will never disappoint you!

—Psalm 27:14 TPT

Waiting is not an idle word. It isn't a word that describes being inactive or a word that permits you to sit around doing absolutely nothing. Mary Magdalene was anything but idle. She ministered day and night to the Lord. Mary valued being close to Jesus more than anything else, and so she waited until He reappeared.

Esther too was a woman who understood the

value of waiting and in return was honoured as queen. During her one year of preparation before being granted an audience with the king, Esther didn't just sit around being pampered—though that was part of her duty, poor thing! Instead, Esther used her time to wisely seek advice concerning the king's desires from Hegai, the king's eunuch, who was in charge of all the women contending for the role of queen. It is quite likely this included researching anything she could learn about the king in order to gain valuable insight on how to impress him above all the other competitors.

And it worked! You see, waiting may suggest stillness, so to some it conjures up a sense of idleness. But waiting is a verb, which means it is actually an action word. There's an expectation or anticipation to waiting for something that requires our eventual *eager* participation when—and only when—God calls for it.

While I was waiting for a book publishing deal, I was busy in preparation. God was preparing me to go to new heights with Him. To do this, He was refining the skills necessary for my future ministry. Specifically, in two areas that would become essential for the ministry into which I was being called. God was also orchestrating something completely new and fresh for the release of my book, though at the time I couldn't see it.

You see, it's important to note that while I was in this season of queen-in-waiting, I couldn't see how God was preparing me or for what He was preparing me. Only in hindsight can I now see what God was doing in that season of my life. The point being that a posture of waiting doesn't always afford you God's vision at the time. It requires trust.

Mary wouldn't have fully known that because she waited at Jesus's empty tomb, the resurrected Messiah would eventually be revealed to her. But she did trust that God had a plan and a purpose in the death of His Son, so she waited expectantly for whatever He had planned next. Likewise, I put my faith in God that He had a plan and purpose for my book and indeed my ministry. So I waited while God prepared me in the meantime.

The first area where God was equipping me was in preaching. This is now one of my greatest joys. But at the time, this was a terrifying undertaking for me as public speaking had always been one of my greatest fears, right up there with my fear of being thrown in a pit of snakes or being stuck in a room full of spiders. I shudder at the thought!

This fear of public speaking surfaced in my teen years after a trying time in English class when other students criticised and made fun of me any time it was my turn to speak. I quickly went from being an A-grade English student to barely passing, and I would do anything in my power to keep from public speaking. So fear of being ridiculed was a very real concern for me. This meant God had some serious work ahead of Him to get me ready and willing to accept my new preaching assignment.

A second area in which God was preparing me during this season of waiting was writing a second book. This doesn't sound so terrifying given I had already completed my first. But that was the point. I couldn't wrap my mind around beginning a second book when my first book had not yet been embraced.

By this time, God had given me the framework for this second book, and I had actually been journaling my conversations with God for the past year. But the notion of stepping into a place of writing and owning my ability as a writer was intimidating. I seriously doubted my abilities. My seeming inadequacies screamed in my face, and self-judgmental thoughts owned much of my cognitive life.

So it was on another morning walk with my Papa that the story of Peter and his famous 'walk on water' moment got me out of my comfort zone, challenging me to step out of the boat and into the realm of possibility. On this particular day, I was having a tug-of-war debate with God, trying to persuade Him that I am not the person He thinks I am. Here I was actually contending with my Creator that I am not a writer and certainly can't overcome a fear of public speaking!

It was while I was sharing with God all my fears and concerns wrapped around my perceived lack of talent that Peter kept coming to mind. I questioned God as to why Peter began to sink even after experiencing the miraculous walk on water (Matthew 14:22-34). Was it only because he'd taken his eyes off Jesus?

The answer I felt God give me on this day was that Peter was doubtful of his ability. He began looking at his circumstances—out on the water walking through the stormy wind and waves to Jesus—through a human lens. In so doing, he stopped trusting in Jesus's own capabilities. He stopped believing that with God all things are possible

(Matthew 19:26).

You see, through a natural human lens, Peter was right. It was ludicrous for him to be doing what he was doing. Human beings can't walk on water. It's physically impossible. We either swim in the water or sink. So once Peter began to look at his circumstances in the natural world, recognising that it was humanly impossible for him to walk on water, fear took over. Doubt began to supersede his earlier conviction that if Jesus said he could do it, then he could do it.

Peter's story highlighted to me something significant in my own walk. Fear was keeping me in the boat. In fact, unlike Peter, I wasn't even willing to get out of the boat and attempt the seemingly impossible. A heap of "but" phrases and rapid-fire excuses were spilling out of my mouth as I continued to debate my point with God.

- But God, I haven't even got a publishing deal for my first book, so why start a second?

- But God, I'm not an author. I just wrote one book out of experience.

- But God, I'm a nobody with no connections.

- But God, I'm tongue-bound and too scared to speak in public.

- But God, who am I to preach to another when I have no credentials?

- But God, maybe I'm not even hearing from you correctly anymore.

But! But! But! My excuses not to write came thick and fast that day, I'm embarrassed to say. Stepping into a preaching role seemed inconceivable. That is, until my endless excuses were both met with one more *but*. Not My will BUT Yours Father (Luke 22:42).

Jesus gave the ultimate *but* in the perfect context. His *but* wasn't the excuse that all of us would have offered God in His circumstances. He didn't want the chalice of death placed upon Him. Who would? He knew the gruesome brutality He was about to face at Calvary. And yet He met the Father with a three-lettered humble, sacrificial conjunction that handed His will over to the Father's come what may: ". . . not My will *but* Yours!"

Lesson learned!

That day as I walked and talked, or more accurately wrestled and tussled with my Papa, I knew at once that I needed to surrender my will to the will of the Father. I needed to trust in the realm of His possibility. I am who He says I am, nothing more, nothing less. If God believes in my abilities, He will heal my hurts, realign my destiny, and begin to prepare, equip, and train me accordingly.

All things are possible through Christ. A phrase reframed by the 1950s actress Audrey Hepburn, who famously put it this way: "Nothing is impossible. The word itself says I'm possible!"

CHAPTER NINE

I have placed before you an open door that no one can shut. I know that you have little strength, yet you have kept my word and have not denied my name.

—Revelation 3:8

I found myself pondering Esther's story in light of my seeming inadequacies, not to mention my many excuses. I think it likely she would have faced similar feelings of unworthiness that in her mind would have disqualified her for the title of queen that she was contending for. I'm sure she must have had many a *but* moment as well. And yet God placed before her an open door that no man could shut.

> I will place on his shoulder the key to the house of David; what he opens no one can shut, and what he shuts no one can open. (Isaiah 22:22)

Though only a young Jewish orphan girl with no real standing to offer the king except perhaps her beauty, Esther was chosen to come into a royal position because God had opened the door for her. He had anointed Esther for such a time as to save her people from annihilation, and all she had to do was submit to the calling on her life.

I've come to see that it's in the surrender, the letting go and trusting in God's plans, that God opens doors on our behalf. Because God gave us free will, God doesn't push His will onto us. Yes, there is God's perfect will. But God wants our permission to fulfil all that He desires in our lives. It is in the relinquishing of full control—"not my will but Yours, Father!"—that our submission to God becomes God having full access to carry out the calling for which He has purposed each of us.

It was almost a year to the date that I'd first submitted my manuscript to the UK Christian publishing house when God revealed to me that the door to that pathway was closed. As you can imagine, I was truly devastated. A year's worth of walking and talking with God flashed through my mind. All I could think was that I clearly mustn't be able to hear God's voice after all. If that wasn't bad enough, I'd obviously also become a crazy person to be seeing lions every day.

And yet the lions continued to come for some time more. It was months later when I realised a change of direction was required. By then, I was in a difficult place with God, doubting my ability to hear from Him, wondering what I had missed, and questioning where I should go from here.

I was also in a conundrum. If I started sending out my manuscript to agents and/or Christian publishing houses globally, I could be years from achieving a publishing deal and from there getting my book into stores. And to my thinking, I'd already wasted a year.

Apart from that, I wasn't sensing God's leading in those options, though admittedly at this point I was questioning my ability to hear the voice of God at all. But it did seem that other writers I spoke with on the subject, whether traditionally published authors or indie authors, were persuading me to go it alone.

At this point, I was nearly a year into my queen-in-waiting season. I could see how God was growing my confidence in areas like preaching and further writing that would become essential for where He was taking my ministry. I could also see that God was placing the right people in my pathway to further my calling. But while these were essential in helping recognise my God-given destiny, it was God's softening of my heart to accept that my ways don't always mean the perfect way that diverted my direction into God's perfect alignment.

You see, God had kept the door closed for traditional publishing because there was a better option for my story to be told. It was only when I was ready for it toward the end of that year of preparation that a new door finally opened up. In fact, it was while I was preparing for my first ever preaching assignment that God showed me one final lion. Not pictorially on this occasion but in a single word.

The topic I'd been asked to preach on was worship.

As I researched that word, I came across a synonym that blew me away—the word lionize. This synonym is sometimes seen in the negative light of idolatry, i.e., placing someone or something unworthy on a pedestal to be adored and fawned over. The verb form would be idolising, or turning into an idol to be worshipped.

But to me, that isn't what the word lionize brings to mind. Rather, it incorporates my absolute heart song and life motto to 'ascribe glory to God and worship Him in the splendour of His holiness' (Psalm 29:2, author's paraphrase). Beyond that, the root of the word lionize is the very image that had defined my entire past year—lion!

Seeing the word lionize during my study on worship changed my perspective completely. I had always thought I needed to go down the traditional publishing path to be taken seriously as a writer. But through one word, it was as if I had been given a new vision, a new purpose, a new calling. And I was immediately excited by new possibilities.

Uncovering the word lionize led to two ministries coming into being at the same time and in God's perfect timing. The first was my first-ever preaching message, which included what God had shown me through that synonym of worship. Secondly, God opened the pathway for me to create my very own self-publishing imprint name: Lionize Press. True to His word, God led me to a publisher with the name lion in it, though I could never have predicted it would be my very own imprint that would publish my first book.

What this year-long experience taught me is that we sometimes need a season of queen-in-waiting. There are lessons to be learned, growth to be had, seeds to be sown, patience to learn, trust and relinquishing required, all during this season of refinement. Queen Esther's testimony reminds us of that. Mary Magdalene also shows us the rewards to be gained in a season of waiting.

We are all purposed with destiny. We each have a calling on our lives. And as the stories of Mary Magdalene, Esther, and even my own journey all testify, the posture of waiting can ultimately lead to receiving great and sometimes unexpected rewards from the Father.

MARY POSTURE

Wait

LESSON # 3: To wait on God and trust in Him is part of an intimate relationship with our Creator. Waiting enables God to orchestrate His plans and purposes for our lives so that we may live out our God-given destiny. Will you surrender to the will of the Father and choose the Mary posture of waiting? Who knows what doors might open up!

What's In Your Hand?

Then the Lord asked him, "What is that in your hand?"

—Exodus 4:2 NLT

DEVOTION OF MY HEART

Ordinary to Extraordinary

Jael, an ordinary tent-dwelling woman with a name that simply means *mountain goat*, was not destined by those around her to be anything out of the ordinary. Jael was not bound for fame or someone you would consider to be extraordinary. Not by human standards anyway.

But God saw what Jael was capable of. He knew what Jael's strengths were, including being well equipped to handle a tent peg. When the enemy of God's people showed up in her tent, God used what was in Jael's hands—a tent peg—to change her destiny and that of God's people (Judges 4).

Jael, or *mountain goat*, became the woman who saved the Israelite nation from brutality. God took the ordinary and brought about something extraordinary by simply using what was in Jael's hands.

CHAPTER TEN

Mountain Goat

He [God] chose what is regarded as insignificant in order to supersede what is regarded as prominent, so that there would be no place for prideful boasting in God's presence.

—1 Corinthians 1:28-29 TPT

I love the women of the Bible. Not just some but all of them. I seem to relate to most of them on some level, scarily so at times. Jael is one woman who may often get overlooked when skimming through all the heroic characters of the Bible. But she has an amazing story to tell and is someone with whom I think many of us women can identify.

Certainly, Jael is someone worth pausing for a moment to reflect on her life. And on one of my many morning walks and talks with God, I did just that. You see, Jael was just your ordinary girl. Someone perhaps much like you or me. She wasn't royalty. She isn't described as having great beauty like Sarah or Rebekah or Esther. She was just a simple country girl who lived her life as a nomadic tent-dweller in the plain of Zaanaim near Kedesh.

Jael's parents mustn't have had very high aspirations for her considering that her name, which in biblical times had significant meaning attached to it, simply means *mountain goat*. I don't know about you, but mountain goat does not sound all that attractive. It sounds common, almost demeaning. Especially in light of biblical women who had gone before her. Take Abraham's wife Sarah, whose name means *princess*. A name given her personally by God to symbolise that she would be a *mother of nations* (Genesis 17:15-16).

If Jael's name is anything to go by, she was destined to simply work the mountainous landscape, tend to the family flocks, and set up tents. Thank God that He turns the ordinary into the extraordinary!

You see, Jael did have some characteristics in common with her namesake that God used to make her extraordinary. Mountain goats live in high altitude up to 14,000 feet above sea level and are well equipped for harsh conditions with a double layer of thick woolly coats that enable them to handle extreme winters. Jael too was equipped and well trained for a difficult task ahead of her.

Mountain goats also have uniquely designed hinds feet that enable them to manoeuvre the rockiest of terrains, most delicate of ledges, and most precarious elevations. In fact, if you just take a moment to Google mountain goats, you'll find some amazing footage of these animals on the most precarious of ledges. Jael too had been provided the right equipment in her hand at the right time.

In short, mountain goats might seem like a common type of animal just as their namesake, Jael, might seem an ordinary woman. But neither the mountain goat nor Jael are anything but extraordinary. Which is why in this section I want to delve deeper into the posture of waiting but this time viewing it from God's vantage point. That is, waiting for God's perfect timing. Since Jael may not be as well-known as other biblical women, let me first recap her story, found in chapter four of the book of Judges.

To set the scene, the Israelites at that time were doing the wrong thing in the eyes of the Lord, so God had sold them into the hands of Jabin, king of Canaan, who reigned in Hazor. Sisera was the commander of Jabin's army, a cruel man who had oppressed the Israelites for twenty years. He was so brutal that the disobedient Israelites began crying out to the Lord for help.

At this time, a woman judge named Deborah was leading the Israelites. She had received a prophecy from God that Sisera and his army would be delivered into the hands of Barak, Israel's own military commander, and ten thousand troops under Barak's command. When Barak insisted on Deborah accompanying him into battle, Deborah was given an additional prophecy that Barak would still be successful but would no longer receive the honour of killing the enemy commander. Instead, God would deliver Sisera into the hands of a woman.

Here enters Jael's heroic moment! While Sisera's army was being annihilated by the Israelite army led by

Barak and Deborah, Sisera managed to flee the scene on foot. He found his way to the tent of an ordinary tent-dweller named Jael, wife of a man named Heber. Heber was allied to Sisera's king, so Sisera assumed Jael would offer him a place of refuge. Let's pick up the story from when Jael meets Sisera.

> Jael went out to meet Sisera and said to him, "Come, my lord, come right in. Don't be afraid." So he entered her tent, and she covered him with a blanket. "I'm thirsty," he said. "Please give me some water." She opened a skin of milk, gave him a drink, and covered him up. "Stand in the doorway of the tent," he told her. "If someone comes by and asks you, 'Is anyone in there?' say 'No.'" But Jael, Heber's wife, picked up a tent peg and a hammer and went quietly to him while he lay fast asleep, exhausted. She drove the peg through his temple into the ground, and he died. Just then Barak came by in pursuit of Sisera, and Jael went out to meet him. "Come," she said, "I will show you the man you're looking for." So he went in with her, and there lay Sisera with the tent peg through his temple—dead.
> (Judges 4:18-22)

I don't know about you, but I find that a pretty gruesome tale. I mean, a tent peg driven through the skull of a man! I'm definitely no expert at setting up a tent, but I do know that hammering a peg into hard ground takes effort. The few times I've helped my husband set up a tent, it has taken me a few good whacks to get the peg to stick in the ground.

So I can't imagine the grit and determination it must have taken Jael to drive the peg through the head of a sleeping man. Nor would this peg have been the size of the average modern camping gear if it went straight through Sisera's head into the ground. Think the long, sharp metal stakes used to pitch a circus or army tent—or even the residential tent of nomadic Bedouin tribal groups.

In summary, God used this ordinary 'mountain goat' for an extraordinary task. But He did so in God's perfect timing. It was in the wait that Jael's destiny and indeed the Israelite nation's destiny was fulfilled. God had been preparing Jael for this moment her entire life. She wasn't just thrown into a situation she couldn't handle. Rather, all the years in preparation mode had led to this victory.

Jael certainly wouldn't have known that God was training her to kill the enemy of His people. Why would she? As far as we know, she wasn't an Israelite since her husband's people were descendants of Moses's wife's family (Judges 4:11) and allies of the king of Hazor. And it's also not like she could have ever predicted that Sisera would come to her tent looking for refuge.

But unbeknownst to Jael, her skill in the art of putting up tents, including how to drive a peg deep into the ground with one quick, hard hit, was exactly the skill God was looking for. Like her name-sake the mountain goat, Jael was well equipped with the right tools to conquer the mountain that lay in front of her. She didn't step outside of her gifting but rather used the skills God had perfected in her over her lifetime.

I think there is a lesson here for us. We are all Jaels,

and her story reminds us that God created us all for a purpose. God has begun and continues to perfect His work in each of us who are God's children (Philippians 1:6). Like Queen Esther, who was not just an orphan girl but exactly who God was looking for to save His people from annihilation. Esther must have had beauty to be chosen as a contestant for the position of queen. But it was her Jewish heritage and a strength of character capable of grabbing the king's attention and swaying his decision-making that God required for the mission to save the Israelite people.

Jael too may have only been a tent-dwelling woman whose name suggests she wasn't expected to amount to anything extraordinary. But she possessed the requisite skills for God to call upon her for an incredible task. This includes the determination and tenacity to follow through when it counted. These qualities were what God was after to bring to justice the enemy that was oppressing the Israelite nation.

Like Esther and Jael, we too are called to rise up as sons and daughters of the highest King and to use what's in our hands, the gifts God has given us, to do His will in conjunction with His perfect timing. We may think that being used profoundly for God's kingdom-building means going to higher levels or being stretched outside our comfort zone. This may well be the case. I am certainly testament to being extended beyond what I am naturally comfortable with insofar as my preaching and writing.

But many times, God is simply calling us to do His will with what is already in our hands. Jael was used by

God in her everyday tent-dwelling skills. You might say that was her talent. Similarly, using our own ordinary daily skills for God's glory as the precious gifts I believe they are, will have a significant kingdom impact.

For some, this may simply mean preparing a meal for someone else. Hospitality may be the gift God wants you to use for His glory. And who knows what amazing opportunities can come from this or the impact your generosity may have on that person's life. You might even have the added blessing of hosting and entertaining an angel unawares as the epistle to the Hebrews reminds us.

> Do not forget to show hospitality to strangers, for by so doing some people have shown hospitality to angels without knowing it. (Hebrews 13:2)

Another example of God simply using what's in our hands for His glory may come from your profession. Perhaps you are a medical professional with a real heart to heal the sick. Then just maybe your actual hands will be the tool God uses to heal those in your care.

There are so many examples throughout the Bible of God using everyday people in everyday situations in extraordinary ways for His glory. A prostitute by the name of Rahab in the city of Jericho comes to mind. You can read how she helped the Israelites conquer that city in the second chapter of the book of Joshua. Then there is Mary, mother to Jesus, another wonderful example we will be looking at more closely of God working divinely through ordinary people.

But let's first look at an even more specific example of God using what was literally in someone's hand to perform the most extraordinary miracles. That person was Moses, and what was in his hand was simply a great big wooden stick.

CHAPTER ELEVEN

God Waits Too

My life, my every moment, my destiny—it's all in your hands.
—Psalm 31:15 TPT

Like Jael, Mary didn't know God was raising her to be someone history would remember, in her case as the most blessed of all mothers (Luke 1:42). She couldn't have known she would bear God's own Son. But God had been waiting for the exact moment in time to bring to fulfilment His promise of a Messiah. He was also waiting for the right vessel through which to fulfil that destiny, and it was through a young Jewish daughter by the name of Mary that we once again see God turning ordinary into the extraordinary.

But there is yet another Bible personage who illustrates God using everyday people for incredible tasks, and that is the story of Moses. Similar to Jael's experience,

God used an ordinary object Moses carried in his hands on a daily basis to perform the miraculous. At this time, Moses had spent almost forty years in the wilderness shepherding his father-in-law's flock of sheep. Then one day, he encounters a bush that won't stop burning and comes face to face with God (Exodus 3-4).

After telling Moses that he was to lead the people of Israel from bondage in Egypt, God asked Moses, "What is that in your hand?"

To which Moses replied, "A staff."

God went on to tell Moses to throw his staff on the ground, upon which it immediately turned into a snake (Exodus 4:3). Almost certainly, Moses never imagined the same staff he'd been using to manage his father-in-law's flocks would one day be used in the most unbelievable acts of wonderment. In fact, his first reaction when God turned his staff into a snake was to run.

But what was simply an ordinary length of wood in Moses's hand became a powerful tool through which God would go on to perform the most incredible miracles on behalf of the Israelite nation, including turning water into blood, parting the Red Sea, and bringing water from a rock.

In the case of both Jael and Moses, God used something with which they were very familiar and skilled to defeat their enemies, conquer the mountains in front of them, and bring glory to our heavenly Father. Jael, Mary, and Moses were also all the result of God's perfect timing and His perfect plan.

For instance, Jael didn't just wake up one day and declare, "Today is the day I'm going to kill Sisera."

Her husband's people were actually at peace with the Canaanites, so she would have been considered an ally to Sisera, not an enemy. Certainly, Sisera must have thought so to take refuge in her tent. But in this situation, it was God who played a major part in choosing Jael to defeat the enemy.

Scripture doesn't tell us why Jael did what she did. But to me, her why is irrelevant. God did what He did, and He waited until He had the perfect host to fulfil His plan. He had been orchestrating this event well before the Israelite judge Deborah prophesied that Sisera would go down at the hand of a woman, and it was no accident that Sisera ended up in Jael's tent.

God was in control then, and God is still in control now. Nothing has changed. We are in God's perfect design today as much as Jael, Esther, Mary, Rahab, and Moses were back then. And yet so often it's hard to get perspective on God's plan and purpose for our lives, especially when we are in the midst of a trial. Or as I termed it in the last section, a queen-in-waiting season.

I live close to the base of Mt. Macedon in Australia's southern state of Victoria. It's only a small mountain, peaking at about 3,000 feet above sea level, so quite a bit shy of our mountain goat's 14,000 feet habitat. About two-thirds up the mountain is a trek locals call the Goat Track. This semi-steep climb takes hikers to a peak where there is a lookout and a twenty-one-meter tall memorial cross.

During Easter one year, my eldest brother Brad and his family, who live in Australia's most northern State, Queensland, came down to stay with my family. Together, we ventured up this Goat Track. Most of the party set off quickly, conquering the trail with relative ease. But my sister-in-law Jen, who was nursing a broken foot, and I lagged behind. We paused regularly and even contemplated heading back down to easier ground.

My brother had left his phone with us. This piece of equipment in our hands showed us the altitude we were at as well as the remaining distance to the peak, which encouraged us to continue on our journey. But we had one other hope that also stirred us on.

I had hiked this trek once before with Jamie, so I knew at one point along the way, the memorial cross that sits at the peak would be visible to us below. And so at every bend, Jen and I looked up. Our hope, our strength came from seeing the cross. Though we didn't have a visual on it for most of our climb, we drew courage from knowing the cross was there. We persevered one (broken-footed for Jen!) step at a time in our pursuit of reaching the cross.

Similarly, even though we can't always see God's plan and purpose for our lives, God is often moving extraordinarily behind the scenes. He is orchestrating something miraculous and out-of-the-box like equipping a woman with skills in hammers and tent pegs to release His people from captivity. No one except maybe the prophet Deborah could have foreseen Jael's involvement in the Israelites' release from oppression. But God's ways and thoughts are far beyond our human comprehension.

Sometimes, like my walk up the Goat Track with my sister-in-law, all that is required of us is to keep walking in the right direction and keep our eyes fixed firmly on the cross of Jesus until God fulfils His work in us as the apostle Paul reminds us.

> He [God] who began a good work in you will carry it on to completion until the day of Christ Jesus. (Philippians 1:6)

There is a work that God has begun in you and me, and He will continue to perfect it in us. He wants us to rise up to be all we have been created to be. He is championing every one of us to be the Jael, Moses, Deborah, or Esther of our world. We were born for such a time as this.

What I find interesting when I look at who God used to defeat Sisera is that He chose someone named after an animal whose qualities were significant to Israelite law. The goat was used by the Israelites as a scapegoat, or substitute, to atone for their sins (Leviticus 16). In Judges 4, we see the Israelites beginning to repent for straying off course and departing from God's law. They begged God for mercy and deliverance from the cruel treatment they were receiving under King Jabin's rule.

In answer to their pleas, God sent them Deborah and Barak. And these two served their purpose. They led the enemy to the right location. But the ultimate victory that brought about a now repentant Israel's deliverance was completed through Jael, whose name means mountain goat, symbolic of repentance from sin. Symbolic as well of a blood sacrifice, which in this case was accomplished as Jael delivered up the blood of Israel's enemy Sisera.

Deborah recognised the significance of Jael's

inclusion in this victory, as we see her later singing Jael's praises.

> Most blessed of women be Jael, the wife of Heber the Kenite, most blessed of tent-dwelling women. (Judges 5:24)

Amazingly, this blessing that Deborah sang of Jael is later echoed by Mary's cousin Elizabeth who was pregnant at the time with John the Baptist.

> When Elizabeth heard Mary's greeting, the baby leaped in her womb, and Elizabeth was filled with the Holy Spirit. In a loud voice she exclaimed: "Blessed are you among women, and blessed is the child you will bear".
> (Luke 1:41-42)

There is a stunning parallel between Jael being the courageous deliverer of victory and redemption to God's people in Canaan and Mary being the courageous mother who delivered the ultimate Deliverer and Redeemer of God's people into this world. A parallel that once again reminds us how God uses the ordinary for the extraordinary in bringing about His ultimate glory.

God also waits for His plans to be fulfilled. He chooses to partner with the right person who has the right tools for the job at hand, and He will then wait to fulfil His plan at His perfect timing. In Jael's testimony and indeed the long-awaited birth of Jesus through Mary, we see that God too models the Mary posture of waiting.

MARY POSTURE

Wait

LESSON # 4: We have all been gifted like Jael with something extraordinary even in the ordinary. God wants to use our gifts for His glory. He has a plan and purpose for each and every one of His children, and He is patiently waiting for His sons and daughters to fulfil their God-given destinies. Will you choose to position yourself in the posture of waiting for God's perfect will to be unveiled? Will you trust in God's timing and wait for His perfect plan to be fulfilled in your life?

I Am Who Christ Says I Am!

For you have acquired new creation life which is continually being renewed into the likeness of the One who created you; giving you the full revelation of God. In this new creation life, your nationality makes no difference, nor your ethnicity, education, nor economic status – they matter nothing. For it is Christ that means everything as He lives in every one of us.

—Colossians 3:10-11 TPT

DEVOTION OF MY HEART

The Transforming Power of God's Glory

God's glory is all around us. Its brilliance resembles a rare and very precious jewel like that of jasper, which is shining and clear as crystal (Revelation 21:11). God's glory is displayed so that we can tangibly see it, feel it, and understand it. We see His glory through rainbows and clouds, in the heavens and on the earth, even through fire and sunlight (Ezekiel 1:28, Exodus 40:34, Psalm 19:1, Numbers 14:21, Exodus 24:17, Habakkuk 3:4).

We can know God's glory intimately and personally through the Son of God, who radiates the Father's glory and expresses the very character of our God (Hebrews 1:3). When we become followers of Jesus, we also reflect God's glory as we become more transformed into Christ's likeness (2 Corinthians 3:18). This is the transforming power of God's glory that is hidden in creation, revealed through Jesus, and mirrored in His glorious and radiant bride (Ephesians 5:27).

CHAPTER TWELVE

Identity

For he knew all about us before we were born and he destined us from the beginning to share the likeness of his Son.

—Romans 8:29 TPT

There's a favourite meme I've seen peddled out on social media from time to time. It shows a picture of a little ginger cat staring at itself in the mirror, only to see the reflection of a lion staring back. I guess for some this meme might represent a false identity. The cat sees itself grander than it ought. It's egocentrism at its best.

But I see the cat looking into a mirror that reflects an image of a lion as actually representing the real truth of who we are. We are, in fact, the mirror image of Jesus, the Lion of Judah (2 Corinthians 3:18, Revelation 5:5). Though we may think we are just ordinary men and women, the truth is that we are His reflection. We are the mirror-image of the Son of God. That makes us extraordinary as Jael's story reminded us in the last section.

Identity is a big topic at the moment, gracing our Australian talkback regularly, particularly for our teens. I assume Australians are not alone when it comes to grappling with knowing who we are and what we have been created to be. I believe it to be a universal struggle.

Personally, I've wrestled with identity issues throughout my life, presenting myself one way to please some people, another way to be liked by others. My identity has sometimes been framed by past criticisms, but it has also been nurtured by praise and promotion. I have seen myself in a mixture of crazy mirrors, not knowing which one is the real me. I have also battled with other people's opinions of who they might perceive me to be in contrast to my own self-esteem.

The truth is that who we are cannot ever be wrapped up in people's perceptions of us, which is partly made up of how much of our true self we want to present in the first place. Nor can our identity be seen through our past criticisms or even our current or former glories.

Who we identify as is not based on any of our triumphs or prior mistakes. It is not found in our gender, career, age, looks, weaknesses, or strengths. It is not based on whether we are married, single, have children, or don't. These only make up part of our life story. Our identity, in actual fact, can only ever be seen in who our Creator says we are.

Identity

God reminded me of this important truth on another series of walks with Him. To know who we are in Christ and what we are called to do is essential if we are to grow in our intimate relationship with our Creator God. When we have mixed views about our identity, we also have a misunderstanding of who we are in Christ. This clouds our ability to *abide* in Him, *wait* on His instruction, then *receive* and move into all He has planned for our lives.

In other words, our identity is linked to our destiny. When we are confused about our own identity, we carry around what I like to call fake identifications. These could be words that we or others have spoken over us throughout our lifetime. Or it could be a belief system, lies from the devil that enslave us and keep us captive from living out our true purpose in Christ.

When we accept these false identifications as truth, we are not stepping into our true identity as a child of God. We are not reflecting Christ's glory as we ought. You see, Scripture tells us that we are Christ's mirror image if we have chosen Jesus as our Lord and Saviour.

> But we all, with unveiled face, beholding as in a mirror the glory of the Lord, are being transformed into the same image from glory to glory, just as by the Spirit of the Lord.
> (2 Corinthians 3:18 NKJV)

So we need to see ourselves in Christ's perfect light. We need to believe in ourselves as righteous, virtuous children of God (2 Corinthians 5:21). We need to accept that we are fearfully and wonderfully made (Psalm

139:14). We need to know and receive the height and depth of God's love for us (Ephesians 3:18) so we can fully embrace that truth and love ourselves in return.

As we saw in an earlier chapter, our heavenly Father doesn't see us in the same light in which we so often see ourselves. God sees us only through the lens of His Son Jesus, who sacrificed His life for us and is perfect in every way. This isn't on an occasional or merit-based ranking. There are no hidden clauses or small-print terms and conditions to how God sees us.

On the contrary, when we surrender our lives to Jesus, our heavenly Father sees us perpetually as unblemished, whole, made in His beautiful image, forgiven, and saved by His grace. Wave after wave, we are washed white as snow through the perfection, righteousness, and holiness that Jesus bought with His own life. His stamp of approval that says 'bought by the blood of the Lamb' is imprinted all over us (Revelation 12:11).

Yet this acknowledgment can be easier said than owned. My own identity in Christ has often been clouded by self-judgment, my thoughts and perceptions framed by negative life experiences. And I know I'm not alone. Many of us carry around fake identifications that hold us back from stepping courageously, confidently, and boldly like Jael did into our God-given calling.

I am thankful for my husband Jamie, who could see I needed some time away to think and write on this subject. In early 2019, he arranged for me to have a few days away from my family and church work at my mother-in-law's holiday unit on a beach that skirts the base of Australia's Victorian coastline. You will have noticed that many of our family vacations and my own spiritual retreats happen by the sea. This is partly because I draw a lot of energy from being close to the ocean. But it is also because a majority of Australians live within an easy drive of our many coastal beachfronts.

As I walked and talked with God along the beach near my mother-in-law's holiday unit, God spoke into this identity issue with me, dispelling many fake identifications I had been carrying around over the years. Insecurities that had defined my life choices. Prejudices I had built up against my age, gender, and qualifications that were holding me back from my God-given purpose and calling. Criticisms I or others had spoken over me that I had inadvertently accepted and now needed to let go. The times I had passed judgment on my body image and other areas in my life I saw as flawed. All of these areas were holding me back from my true identity in Christ.

God also showed me just how heavy my load had been as I carried around all these lies and untruths about myself. A burden the Father wanted me to lay down at His feet. This burden is carried by too many of God's precious children, but God wants to release each of us. Instead, as the popular gospel song suggests, the Father wants us to 'cast our burdens unto Jesus'.

God is inviting us to remove our heavy yokes of fake identifications and leave them at His altar. In exchange, He is inviting us to pick up the one identification tag that truthfully defines who we are in Christ. That identification simply reads: "I am who He says I am."

When I consider the three Marys in regards to the topic of identity, Mary the mother of Jesus comes immediately to mind. Since she wasn't yet married when she became pregnant through the Holy Spirit, Mary could have been as young as thirteen years of age when she gave birth to Jesus by the cultural norms of her day. The small Galilean village of Nazareth where she grew up was by no means the Beverly Hills of its day. In fact, it was so insignificant that one of Jesus's disciples asked when first told of Jesus, "Can anything good come from Nazareth?" (John 1:46 NLT)

Nor were Mary's parents in any way prominent that we know. That they had betrothed her to a village carpenter would suggest a very ordinary station in life. When the angel informed Mary that she would give birth to God's Son, it isn't surprising her first reaction was to become greatly troubled and afraid (Luke 1:29). I'm sure she wondered why a simple village girl would be chosen for such a highly favoured assignment.

I can almost hear Satan whispering doubt and self-criticism into Mary's ears. Perhaps he plagued her cognitive world with thoughts of inadequacies and inferiorities based around her upbringing, age, or perceived insignificance. Lies the enemy loves to speak over us as well to prevent us from walking out our true God-given destiny.

Thank God our Lord doesn't see us in the same light as we so often see ourselves and by which Satan tries to keep us limited and even bound. As with Jael, God

Identity

once again demonstrates to us through Mary's story that He uses the ordinary for the extraordinary. Something the apostle Paul also recognised.

> God chose the foolish things of the world to shame the wise; [he] chose the weak things of the world to shame the strong. (1 Corinthians 1:27)

In that critical identity moment when Mary was 'deeply troubled over the words of the angel and bewildered over what this may mean for her' (Luke 1:29, TPT), she was quickly reassured of her true identity by the angel of the Lord.

> Do not yield to your fear, Mary, for the Lord has found delight in you and has chosen to surprise you with a wonderful gift. (Luke 1:30 TPT)

How glorious that God reassures us when fear and doubt wants to squash us from entering into our true calling. How breath-taking that when the enemy tries to hold us back from reaching our God-given potential, the Lord will often send a messenger to encourage us. I've certainly been recipient of many a timely word of encouragement from a friend, a Scripture, or a prophetic word, each evidence of God communicating His love once again to His beloved children.

In Mary's situation, the angel gave her a word in season to help her not yield to her fears or allow the temptation of self-criticism and self-doubt to take over.

Instead, she was encouraged to surrender to the Father's will and see herself through His eyes—delightful, chosen, and gifted. She is who He says she is. And that includes becoming mother to the Son of God.

So often we see ourselves in the wrong mirror. Like the crazy mirrors I mentioned earlier, all our earthly influences, both positive and negative, frame our mindset. Our childhood perceptions. The life choices we have made. The comments and criticisms we have received and taken to heart. Our memories. All of these have played a part in creating an image of how we see ourselves as well as how we have allowed others to perceive us. More often than not, that image is not an accurate representation at all.

In the next chapter, I'd like to address those negative lies that hold us back from our true identity as God's children. If we are to live out our God-given destiny and receive our true inheritance as sons and daughters of the Most High King, we must first take captive every thought that is opposite to Christ's truth. Just as the angel encouraged Mary, we must insist that every wrong belief system, lie, and negative statement that enters our mind bow in obedience to the Anointed One, Jesus Christ our Lord, as the apostle Paul puts it so well.

> We demolish arguments and every pretension that sets itself up against the knowledge of God, and we take captive every thought to make it obedient to Christ.
> (2 Corinthians 10:5)

CHAPTER THIRTEEN

Power Of The Tongue

Death and life are in the power of the tongue, and those who love it and indulge it will eat its fruit and bear the consequences of their words.

—Proverbs 18:21 AMP

I'm sure most of us have spoken negatively about our identity at some point in our life. Some perhaps more so than others. God has chastised me on numerous occasions for the words I've spoken that have produced death rather than life, as the above proverb tells us our words can do. So in this chapter I want to address the words we speak over ourselves and even others in view of the truth of who we are in Christ. James in his New Testament epistle writes:

> With the tongue we praise our Lord and Father, and with it we curse human beings, who have been made in God's

likeness. Out of the same mouth come praise and cursing. My brothers and sisters, this should not be. (James 3:9-10)

James is telling us here that our speech has power that can be used for good or for evil, for blessing or cursing. In fact, he compares an uncontrolled tongue to a hellish fire, calling it 'the sum of wickedness' and 'the most dangerous part of our human body' (James 3:6, TPT). In other words, there is such power in what we declare that it can either produce an abundance of fruitful life or it can produce death, poverty, and scarcity. This is why it is so vital that our speech always be safeguarded.

Many times throughout my life, I have found myself naively but no less dangerously speaking words contrary to the truth of who Jesus says I am, such as: "I'm afraid . . . I can't forgive myself . . . It's impossible for me . . . I feel all alone . . . No one cares about me . . . I'm not smart . . . I'm a nobody . . . I'm unlovable . . . I'm ugly . . . I hate my body . . . I can't . . . I'm not worthy."

Do any of these sound familiar to you? Such negative words that we or others have spoken over us throughout our lifetime have been our accusers. These and so many other lies have the power to wrongfully define and limit us. Declarations we've inadvertently made that are just not true hold us back from being all we were created to be.

During the first five years of my nine-year faith journey to have a baby, I found myself saying words like "I can't have children . . . I'm infertile. . . I'll never be a mum . . . I'm doomed to childlessness."

Foolishly, I aligned myself with the deceiver of this world by speaking such curses over my body. Words contrary to who Christ says I am and for which I had to repent, renounce, and seek restoration. You can read my prayer of confession over these lies in my first book *Having Faith*.

On another occasion, I naively but no less wrongfully spoke negative words that ended up having a powerful effect on my youngest child. The words I was speaking weren't directed towards me or even my unborn son. Nevertheless, they were harmful. I'd been diagnosed with extremely low iron levels, but I was also exhausted with life in general. I was busy helping Jamie to get our new construction company off the ground. I was heavily engaged in prayer ministry. I was absorbed in writing my first draft of *Having Faith*. I was also extremely busy running after our two active toddlers, both under four years of age.

Suffice it to say, I was acting more like Martha than Mary in this season of life. Instead of abiding and resting in my final pregnancy, I was fatigued, impatient, and intolerant, and my words reflected that overwhelmed state of exhaustion.

Maybe my busy lifestyle warranted some sympathy. It certainly evoked self-pity in me! But none of these lifestyle decisions justified my negative words. I had a choice in how busy my life was. And I didn't choose the better Mary option of abiding at the feet of Jesus.

When my third child Levi was finally born, he experienced symptoms of colic. This included crying for long periods of time. Furthermore, he was so attached to me he wouldn't go to anyone else or sleep on his own (ironically, the name Levi means 'joined' or 'united').

One evening, about a month after Levi's birth, Jamie and I were praying about Levi's symptoms when God showed me the truth of the matter. He showed me ever so graciously, as is our Lord's way, that the negative words I'd spoken over my pregnancy were interpreted in-utero by my son as his not being wanted. Fear of abandonment or rejection was the result. This fear caused him to cling to my side and cry unceasingly when left alone.

As you can imagine, I was deeply distressed when the Spirit of the Lord showed me that my words were the root cause of my child's infantile colic and attachment issues. I'm not at all suggesting this is the cause for every child with colic. But in my case, it was a most devastating truth for which I had to bear the consequence.

Thank God, His truth sets us free (John 8:32). The moment God revealed this to me, I sought forgiveness and healing for Levi. That very night, my son was completely healed of all colic symptoms. He began allowing others to care for him and was content to be left on his own.

Satan is the ultimate liar. He wants to keep us stuck in false identifications. He delights in seeing us self-harm through deathly words or by flippantly speaking out untruths that can have a huge impact on our own life or someone else's, as I discovered through my pregnancy with Levi.

The devil will have us believe in false truths so we won't feel worthy to be all God has created us to be. We are promised abundant life through Jesus. In complete contrast, Satan comes to steal, kill, and destroy (John 10:10). He will always try to block us from our true destiny which comes with complete authority as children of God.

I have no doubt Satan would have tried to keep Mary from accepting God's extraordinary calling on her life. Mary's destiny as mother to the Messiah came with incredible authority. She was called for such a time as to bring forth the Son of God. Though a great privilege for Mary, it also carried a great weight of responsibility. God hand-picked Mary for this unique assignment because He knew her true identity and had destined her from the beginning of time to become the mother of His only begotten Son.

Our destiny comes with purpose and authority as well, and it is for such a time as now that we are to receive it. I mentioned in an earlier chapter that abiding in Jesus means to also abide in the Word of God. They are one and the same because Jesus is the Word of God (John 1:1). Likewise, our true identity is revealed through Jesus the Word. The mirror God places in front of us to show us our true reflection as the mirror image of His Son Jesus is, in fact, the Word of God.

> If you listen to the Word and don't live out the message you hear, you become like the person who looks in the mirror of the Word to discover the reflection of his face in the beginning. You perceive how God sees you in the mirror of the Word, but then you go out and forget your divine origin.

> But those who set their gaze deeply into the perfecting law of liberty are fascinated by and respond to the truth they hear and are strengthened by it – they experience God's blessing in all that they do! (James 1:23-25 TPT)

For every false identification the accuser would have us believe, there is a Scripture in God's life-giving manual, the Bible, that tells the real truth of who we are in Jesus. When we accept these Scriptures as truth, we are choosing to hear the voice of God over our lives instead of Satan's.

For instance, we might say, "I'm afraid." But God puts the Bible in front of us and says, "No, child, I have not given you a spirit of fear. I have given you a spirit of love and self-discipline" (2 Timothy 1:7, author's paraphrase).

When we don't feel able to forgive ourselves, God says, "Beloved, I sent my Son Jesus to atone for your sins. You are forgiven, so walk in that freedom" (Ephesians 1:7, author's paraphrase).

When we struggle to believe in the seemingly impossible, God tells us, "Nothing is impossible through Christ Jesus who loves you" (Luke 18:27, author's paraphrase).

When we feel alone and abandoned, God reminds us that He "will never leave us nor forsake us" (Hebrews 13:5, author's paraphrase). When the accuser tells us we are ill-equipped, unqualified, or not smart enough, God reminds us that He will "supply us with godly wisdom" (1 Corinthians 1:30, author's paraphrase).

For those of us who have felt or been accused of

being useless, lacking any form of ability, feeling like a nobody, God again places His mirror, the Bible, in front of us and says, "You are My child. You are a prince or princess of the highest King" (Galatians 3:26, author's paraphrase).

Even when we feel nobody loves us, God is there to remind that He loves each one of us "with an everlasting love" (Jeremiah 31:3). And in those moments when we don't think we are attractive and comparisons set in, God wants all of us to know that we are 'fearfully and wonderfully made' in God's own perfect image (Psalm 139:14, Genesis 1:27).

Do you see the difference? Where Satan speaks lies over our identity, Jesus reveals Himself through the truth of His Word. This is God speaking directly to us. It is so important for us to know and accept who we are in Christ Jesus so that we can then live out our true calling as a son and daughter of the living God. This is where our victory lies.

By abiding in, waiting upon, and receiving the truth of our identity, which is found only through Jesus and in His Word, we can take up our true position as a child of God's. We can then accept that we are heirs according to His promises (Galatians 3:26, 29). And part of our heirship is intimacy with our heavenly Father, our Garden of Eden heritage.

As in Jael's story, we need to be confident in who we have been created to be. Had Jael waivered in her true identity, she may have missed out on the opportunity to be used in a mighty and powerful way for God. Perhaps Israel would not have been set free at the hand of the woman

God had selected.

Likewise, Mary may not have received the utmost privilege of becoming mother to the Son of God and most blessed of all women had she insisted, "I'm a nobody. I can't. I'm too young, I'm nothing but a Nazarene. Nothing good comes from here."

Knowing and owning our true identity in Christ is paramount. Just as in Jael's era or Mary's, it is crucial that we rise up, look in the mirror, and see ourselves not as that little ginger cat in the meme picture but as the reflection of the Lion of Judah. It is time to take off the false identifications by which Satan has had us bound and put on instead the one true identification tag that speaks this truth: "I am who He says I am."

Once we've owned and believed the truth about our identity, which is found only in Jesus and His Word, then we can embrace our true calling as God's child and decree as Mary did when told she would be mother to the Son of God:

> "I am the Lord's servant," Mary answered. "May your word to me be fulfilled." (Luke 1:38)

MARY POSTURE

Receive

LESSON # 5: As believers in Christ, we find our identity only in who He says we are. In fact, as God's children created in His very likeness, we reflect as a mirror-image the Son of God. Will you choose to accept this truth that you are delightful, chosen, and gifted? Will you remove the false identifications that have held you back and instead posture yourself to know the truth of who you are in Christ, then ready yourself to step into all for which God has purposed you?

Then One Day

If I could touch even his clothes, I know I will be healed.

—Mark 5:28 TPT

DEVOTION OF MY HEART

Our Father At Work Everyday

As I was walking along my country lane one day, I noticed something I hadn't seen before. Where sunlight shone down over the road, the thin lines of thousands upon thousands of spider webs could be seen weaving their way across the gravelled road. Not visible without bright light and too delicate to be felt, these intricately-woven silk-like threads lining my pathway reminded me that God is working tirelessly behind the scene of our own lives beyond what we can see or feel. Unseen in the background, it is He who orchestrates those 'suddenly' or 'then one day' God-encounters.

CHAPTER FOURTEEN

God Encounters

Suddenly, a woman came from behind Jesus and touched the tassel of his prayer shawl for healing.
—Matthew 9:20 TPT

When my daughter Faith was in her primary years, she loved to write stories, often for hours at a time, enthusiastically reciting her latest masterpiece to her family as she went along. Faith's stories even became a bit of a highlight amongst her classmates as they anticipated the latest edition of her Girl's Lab adventure stories. One thing I found of interest in my ten-year-old's storytelling was that whenever something new and exciting was about to enter the story, Faith would typically start off with one of two phrases that almost always ended with multiple exclamation marks:

- Suddenly . . . !!!
- Then one day . . . !!!

God encounters are often like that too. I have had many 'suddenly' and 'then one day' moments that have left me in awe and wonder of my Creator God. These moments have almost always come out of a season of abiding and waiting, which then produce some sort of receiving. None more so than when I found out I was pregnant after my nine-year faith journey to have a baby.

Apart from being my dad's birthday, January 22, 2006, is forever etched as the greatest 'then one day' God-moment of my life. As I looked at the double lines on my pregnancy stick that told me I was finally going to be a mum after such a long journey, I was overwhelmed with awe. It was quite a powerful moment in time and definitely worthy of a thousand exclamation marks.

The Bible teems with these suddenly and then one day examples. Abraham's wife Sarah was past her child-bearing years, having already entered into menopause. Then one day, Sarah miraculously conceived (Genesis 21:2). Saul encountered Jesus suddenly on the road to Damascus, diverting his murderous attacks against followers of Christ and realigning him to become one of Jesus's most devout followers and a father of the early Christian church (Acts 9:3-6).

Moses too had a then one day encounter with God at a burning bush, which repurposed his destiny as leader of the Israelite nation (Exodus 3). A demon-troubled woman named Mary Magdalene had her own then one day encounter with Jesus, during which she was made whole, washed clean, and became a brand-new creation in Christ (Luke 8:2). Yes, you will never be the same after a suddenly or then one day encounter with God.

Another woman in the Bible had the extraordinary combination of a then one day encounter with Jesus followed by a suddenly she was healed moment (Matthew 9:20-22; Mark 5:25-34; Luke 8:43-48). Her story has some parallels to Mary Magdalene's story. Mary was undoubtedly shunned because of the demonic influences over her life. This woman has no name in Scripture except that of the woman with 'the issue of blood'. But she too endured isolation for twelve long, lonely years due to a constant bleeding condition.

Apart from the exhaustion and other physical suffering such an affliction would have caused (I can't imagine how iron-deficient she must have been!), this woman would have been considered ceremonially unclean by the standards of the Levitical law (Leviticus 15:19-29). This would have made her an outcast, marginalised by her society.

Everything in her life would have been difficult. Normally, a woman was considered unclean only during the seven days of her monthly menstruation cycle (Leviticus 15:19) and therefore isolated from the rest of the community. But since her condition had not ceased for twelve years, she would have been barred from the synagogue and any other public interaction. Even offering a sacrifice to atone for her sins, also part of Levitical law, was not permissible as long as she was unclean.

She also could not have marital relations with her husband while she was still bleeding as that would make him unclean (Leviticus 15:24). So if she was married, her husband would have every right to divorce her for 'non-performance' (Deuteronomy 24:1). Another possible stain to her name as the divorced woman with the issue of blood!

This woman had spent all she had on the best available medical treatments. But instead of better, she was getting worse (Mark 5:26). Life was dismal, and she must have felt great unworthiness and shame. Every aspect of her circumstances would have left her feeling alone, abandoned, unwanted, unloved, a blemish to her society. Her illness may have very likely been seen as a result of a sin that she or some family member must have committed (John 9:1-3).

Can you imagine feeling that unclean? Having no one to turn to in your suffering? Having nowhere to go without a stigma following you? Not being able to touch another human being for twelve long and lonely years because you were deemed impure and unclean? Having to remain in perpetual isolation?

We had a small taste of isolation during the Covid-19 pandemic that stormed our globe in 2020. While marginal compared to what the woman with the issue of blood would have endured, the loneliness of isolation was nevertheless experienced by millions as we were forced into months of lock-down, only allowed out of our homes for essential services. Throughout Australia and many other countries, social distancing regulations and face masks were mandatory. Strict curfews were in place for weeks at a time while contact with anyone outside immediate family was prohibited. Failure to comply could result in fines or even jail.

This woman with the issue of blood had to adhere to social distancing on a far larger scale, forced into a jail-like isolation sentence for twelve lonely years, weighed down with rejection and abandonment. I can just imagine the false identifications she must have owned in her state of isolation, the lack of self-worth, acceptance, and love. The lies about her true identity would have been a heavy, unforgiving burden to carry. All hope for this woman known only for her condition seemed lost.

Then one day when this woman was at her wit's end, hope was restored. Jesus, whom people called the Healer, of whose miraculous deeds she'd heard so many accounts, had arrived in her hometown. Suddenly, a surge of faith and belief arose within her. As she pushed through the crowd that day, defying all societal and religious sanctions, this woman's focus was on one thing and one thing alone—an encounter with Jesus. Repeatedly she said to herself:

> If I could touch even his clothes, I know I will be healed.
> (Mark 5:28 TPT)

She didn't care who she might offend as she fought through the jostling crowd for a position just close enough to touch Jesus's cloak. As she stretched out her hand, somehow her fingers managed to take hold of the edge of Jesus's tunic. It was just for an instant, but that was enough. The moment she touched Jesus's clothing, she felt a shift in her body, as did Jesus.

> Jesus knew at once that someone had touched him, for he felt the power that always surged around him had [suddenly] passed through him for someone to be healed. (Mark 5:30 TPT)

A God encounter will have powerful impact. Not only did this woman have a then one day encounter with Jesus that healed her physically from twelve years of haemorrhaging, but she was suddenly made ceremonially clean again. Jesus could have condemned this woman for touching Him in her unclean state. Any other person, particularly a Pharisee, would likely have done so. But in typical Jesus fashion, He overturned the Levitical law forbidding her from touching Him in her unclean state, not only making her clean and pure again internally but publicly commending her tenacious act of faith, thus making her clean before all her peers.

> Daughter, because you dared to believe, your faith has healed you. Go with peace in your heart, and be free from your suffering! (Mark 5:34 TPT)

In and through Jesus, we are made whole. We are set free. We are a new creation, holy, forgiven, and unblemished. We are completely and gloriously washed clean. Just as Mary Magdalene became one of Jesus's most loyal followers after her healing and was honoured to become the first to see the resurrected Jesus after faithfully positioning herself to wait at His tomb (John 20:16), so this woman referenced only as the one with 'the issue of blood' was immortalised in Scripture because of her incredible and tenacious act of faith.

By waiting for her encounter, then abiding just close enough to touch Jesus's cloak, this woman positioned herself to receive. The three Mary postures in full action. Had she given up along the journey, the healing Jesus wanted to offer may not have come to pass. But because she persevered and ran the race marked out for her (Hebrews 12:1-3), she suddenly and then one day received instant healing after twelve long years of haemorrhaging.

Oh, how God bestows 'a crown of beauty instead of ashes' (Isaiah 61:1-3)! God-encounters will always produce breath-taking then one day and/or suddenly moments all worthy of a thousand exclamation marks!!!!!!

CHAPTER FIFTEEN

God Of The Eleventh Hour

The Lord your God, who is going before you, will fight for you.

—Deuteronomy 1:30

While out walking and talking with God one morning, I began recounting the numerous *suddenly* and *then one day* moments I'd had in my own life where God has intervened in seemingly impossible scenarios. As I contemplated these stories of God's unending faithfulness, I was overwhelmed with tears by just how awesome our God truly is. He really is the God of the seemingly impossible. He is the God who orchestrates the most extraordinary outcomes in what seem the bleakest situations.

The woman with the issue of blood we just read about is a testament to that. It wasn't chance that Jesus just happened to be in her hometown that day. His positioning and timing are always perfect in every way. Even when all hope seemed lost, the God of the eleventh hour, as He is sometimes affectionately referenced, came through.

This was definitely the case on one occasion in 2004 when God showed up at the last moment. I was the overseeing director of a non-profit welfare centre in an urban area about a half-hour's travel from where I currently reside in the Victoria countryside. As a non-profit, we relied heavily on grants and donations to run our programs. But it was through the governing body of the church denomination Jamie and I attended that our facility and utilitarian costs were paid. Unfortunately, the host church had fallen on financial hardship, so the work funds they contributed to cover the rent were quickly becoming depleted.

I knew this centre was at the heart of God's restorative plan for the local community as it ministered to thousands of people through food relief, financial assistance, subsidised Christian counselling, a connect group for people with intellectual disabilities as well as a thriving youth group. But I also knew it was going to require a miracle to keep our doors open. For many months, our intercessory prayer team prayed for God's intervention, but in the natural realm, nothing seemed to shift. God had given me one Scripture to hold onto during this time, which gave the team a glimmer of hope:

God of the Eleventh Hour

> Be still [wait] and know that I am God; I will be exalted among the nations, I will be exalted in the earth.
> (Psalm 46:10)

This Scripture sustained us for a time. But as the months rolled on, it was difficult to see how a positive outcome could be possible. Staff and volunteers were increasingly discouraged. That is until we had our suddenly and then one day moment.

It was quite literally at the eleventh hour that God showed up as we were just days away from closing shop. I was finalising some paperwork and packing up my office when a woman knocked on the centre's front door. We were already shut to the public, and I'd told the team to redirect any callers elsewhere so we could concentrate on packing. But even though a volunteer tried to move this person along, she was insistent on meeting with me.

Begrudgingly, I am now embarrassed to say, I invited the woman into my office. My hope was to brush her off quickly so I could get back to the piles of paperwork that needed completing before the close-down deadline. But it was at that moment when I least expected it and deserved it even less that the God of the eleventh hour showed up. Through the organisation she represented, the woman began detailing a proposal for sharing the building, including a rental agreement that was just shy of what we were currently paying with a proposed two-year contract to boot.

Moreover, her organisation would be happy for us to continue operating all our ministries out of the building. They were only interested in utilising two rooms, amazingly, both of these rooms we rarely used, plus sharing the kitchen and bathroom with us.

Talk about a miracle! I couldn't believe what I was hearing. You just can't orchestrate that sort of God-encounter. Not only would the welfare centre be able to remain in operation, but we could do it in total financial freedom, allowing all our funds to go into community outreach. This would also unburden our governing church body from their financial hardship. Had we not listened to God's direction to be still and wait on Him, we would have missed out on this incredible blessing. We would have also failed to allow God to be exalted as He so deserved.

Sometimes God-encounters require us to just be still and know that He is God. I.e., the Mary posture of waiting, as my welfare centre story illustrates. Other times we may need all three Mary postures to be in action as the woman with the issue of blood can testify. But regardless of which, we can be sure of one thing. God is working tirelessly behind the scene on our behalf.

God is the guardian for His people and never slumbers nor sleeps (Psalm 121:4). He may seem like the God of the eleventh hour. But every day our Father is magnificently and intricately working in the background of each of our lives—sometimes to bring about the most extraordinary suddenly and then one day headlines in our very own life stories!

MARY POSTURE

Abide, Wait, and Receive

LESSON # 6: Are you waiting for your suddenly or then one day moment? Our heavenly Father works tirelessly in the background of our lives, and He will always show up at exactly the right hour, even when it looks like the eleventh hour. Will you choose to abide close enough to your Saviour to hear His plans for your life? Will you linger a little longer in the posture of waiting in readiness to receive the hope you profess?

Unveiled for More of His Glory

> We can all draw close to him with the veil removed from our faces. And with no veil we all become like mirrors who brightly reflect the glory of the Lord Jesus.
> —2 Corinthians 3:18 TPT

DEVOTION OF MY HEART

More of Your Glory

When Moses came down from Mount Sinai after having spent time in God's presence, his face shone so brightly from the glory of God that he had to place a veil over his face because the Israelites couldn't look at his brightly-lit face (Exodus 34:29-35). As time went on, the brightness would begin to fade, so he would remove his veil and present himself again before the Lord, as if to say, "More, God! I want more of Your glory!"

Each time he entered God's presence, God would 'top up' his fading brightness, and Moses's face would once again radiate brightly the glory of God.

This is where the bride of Christ stands too. Just as Moses experienced, there is an intimacy that God is seeking. Moses was considered a friend of God (Exodus 33:11), and that same intimate relationship is what God desires with us as well.

It is time to enter a close, intimate relationship with the Lord. It is time to present ourselves before the Lord with unveiled faces, and say as Moses said, "More, God! I want more of Your glory!"

CHAPTER SIXTEEN

Mount Sinai Encounter Sanctuary

So the Lord spoke to Moses face to face, as a man speaks to his friend.

—Exodus 33:11 NKJV

One morning back in 2012 when my middle child was about four years of age, Joel made a rather intriguing request. He asked me to wash his pyjamas so they would be clean for when he went to bed that night. As you might imagine, I asked him why the urgency for clean pyjamas. Above all, why on earth did he need them to be ready for that night?

In Joel's typical matter-of-fact, nonchalant kind of response, my older son simply stated that he had met Jesus on the previous night. He'd been wearing dirty pyjamas so tonight he wanted to have clean nightwear on in case Jesus came to visit him again.

I don't know which part surprised and excited me more—that Jesus had communed with my son, seemingly face-to-face, or that Joel was so expectant of a second visitation he was almost blasé about the possibility of Jesus returning that night. Whatever the case, this personal exchange my son had with the Son of God got me thinking about how completely non-discriminatory intimate encounters with God are. Jesus said in the Gospel of Matthew:

> Let the little children come to me, and do not hinder them, for the kingdom of heaven belongs to such as these. (Matthew 19:14)

Jesus is inviting everyone into relationship with Him. There is no bias or hierarchy involved. In fact throughout Jesus's ministry, we see Him embrace and even promote marginalised people. The woman caught in adultery comes to mind. Instead of casting the first stone, Jesus provoked onlookers to evaluate their own prejudices by first looking at the sins in their own lives.

> Let any one of you who is without sin be the first to throw a stone at her. (John 8:7)

Mary of Bethany's extravagant act of worship when she poured out costly perfume to anoint Jesus is another example of Jesus interceding on behalf of those others belittle. We will look at this in more detail later, but instead of reprimanding Mary for what His own disciples and others were calling wasteful extravagance, Jesus quite firmly addressed the slander spoken against Mary and publicly commended her extravagant act of love and devotion.

The apostle Paul addressed a similar sentiment in what I dub his 'all-inclusive non-prejudicial' speech not so dissimilar to civil rights activist Martin Luther King, Jr's famous 'I have a dream' plea for unity to the American nation in 1963. In Paul's address to the Galatian church, he too was seeking oneness.

> There is neither Jew, nor Gentile, neither slave nor free, nor is there male and female, for you are all one in Christ Jesus.
> (Galatians 3:28)

What Paul is saying here is that there is no bias when it comes to communing with God. We are all one in Him. My son's age did not preclude him from spending alone time with Jesus. In fact in a fascinating twist, I was attending a Bible study years later when another mother shared the exact same testimony of how her daughter, who at a similar age as my son, also encountered Jesus in the same way as Joel did. This young girl had also asked her mother for a clean pair of pyjamas in case Jesus visited again the next night. It seems Jesus is very particular with our children's clean nightwear!

The peculiarity of wanting clean pyjamas does have some biblical precedence as God also asked the Israelites to wash and consecrate themselves before He came down from Mount Sinai to commune with them (Exodus 19:9-11). But what God proved to me through these two young children is that He does not discriminate. God's invitation to spend time in His presence is an invitation for all of us as God proclaimed through the Old Testament prophet Joel.

> I will pour out my Spirit on all people. Your sons and daughters will prophesy, your old men will dream dreams, your young men will see visions. Even on my servants, both men and women, I will pour out my Spirit in those days. (Joel 2:28-29)

Encounters with God are for everyone. In the last section, we looked at God-encounters through suddenly and then one day moments that all have to do with God showing up when we least expect it. His timing is perfect. We can count on God arriving exactly on time, never early and never late.

In this next section, I want to go deeper into what it looks like to have unveiled encounters with God and receive a greater measure of His glory out of our intimate union with Christ. I want to draw a parallel to the friendship Moses enjoyed with God, which came about through applying similar principles to our three Mary postures. I also want to illustrate how we are designed for our very own Mount Sinai encounters, which includes intimate communion with our Creator similar to and even in greater measure than what Moses experienced.

Mount Sinai Encounter Sanctuary

Scripture shows us that Moses had incredible encounters with God in a place called Mount Sinai. While on this mountain top, Moses chose to abide continuously in the presence of God. He chose to wait for divine revelation and impartation. In fact, Moses abided and waited on multiple occasions for forty days and forty nights in a posture of fasting (Deuteronomy 9), something later replicated by Jesus Himself when He spent forty days and nights in the wilderness (Matthew 4:2).

Out of those first two Mary postures of abiding and waiting, Moses went on to receive three outcomes. He received God's calling on his life, which was to lead the Israelites out of captivity and into the Promised Land (Exodus 3). He received words to live by—the Ten Commandments, which were handed to him on Mount Sinai. He also received an impartation of God's glory wherein his face radiated so brightly he had to cover it with a veil because no one could stand to look upon the brightness (Exodus 34:28-35).

By exercising the three Mary postures of abiding, waiting, and receiving, Moses communed with the Lord over and again. Mount Sinai, where all of Moses's early encounters took place, became his 'encounter sanctuary,' the place where he would meet with God face-to-face. Later on, he also communed with God in the tabernacle God instructed him to build.

This encounter sanctuary and indeed the friendship Moses enjoyed with God (Exodus 33:11) is still available to us today but in even greater measure through our intimate union with Jesus. The apostle Paul shows us that the former glory Moses received from God on Mount Sinai and in the tabernacle (friendship, encounter, impartation) is nothing in comparison to the greater measure of glory we receive through the Son of God and His Spirit living within us today.

> Now if the ministry that . . . was engraved in letters on stone [the Ten Commandments] came with glory, so that the Israelites could not look steadily at the face of Moses because of its glory, transitory though it was, . . . how much greater is the glory of that which lasts! Therefore, since we have such a hope, we are very bold. We are not like Moses, who would put a veil over his face to prevent the Israelites from seeing the end of what was passing away. But their minds were made dull, for to this day the same veil remains when the old covenant is read. It has not been removed, because only in Christ is it taken away . . . Now the Lord is the Spirit, and where the Spirit of the Lord is, there is freedom. And we all, who with unveiled faces contemplate the Lord's glory, are being transformed into his image with ever-increasing glory, which comes from the Lord, who is the Spirit. (2 Corinthians 3:7-18)

Paul is saying here that a far more excellent glory than the fading ministry Moses encountered is available to all believers. And unlike Moses, who used a veil to hide God's glory from the fearful Israelites, the veil was lifted from us the moment we were joined to our Messiah, Jesus.

With that veil removed, we can easily draw close to God. In doing so, we become like mirrors that brightly reflect the glory of the Lord Jesus and are constantly being transfigured into His very image as we move from one ever-increasing level of glory to another. This is amazing news!

The former law, or 'old covenant' that Moses received, also had restrictions and limitations. In contrast, we have complete freedom in Christ. In other words, the access we have to the Father is unhindered. Our Mount Sinai encounters are not a one-off occurrence nor isolated to a location as Moses experienced. They are not just for the elite or in Moses's case for God's spokespeople. No matter who we are, where we are, or where we are going, we can spend time in God's presence as believers of Christ. There is no prejudice.

The late American Christian pastor and author A.W. Tozer put it this way: "Worshipers never leave church; we carry our sanctuary wherever we go."

This means that for worshipers and followers of Jesus, our veil has been permanently lifted. We carry His presence wherever we go because God's Spirit is dwelling within us. Moses hid his radiant face under a veil. But when he came into God's presence, he would uncover his face as if to say, "God, give me more of Your glory. I can't live without it."

In response, God would top up the level of glory on Moses's face to the point that he would have to re-cover his face in front of the other Israelites because it shone so brightly (Exodus 34:34-35). But for us, no veil is needed because of our union with Christ. And with no veil, we reflect the glory of the Lord Jesus Christ constantly. Nor does that glory fade as Moses's did. When we abide in Jesus, He abides in us (John 15:4) and His glory that lives within us is forever brightly lit. That glory continues to grow brighter as we are perpetually transformed into our Saviour's likeness.

I remember on my wedding day when the minister pronounced Jamie and me as husband and wife. With a twinkle in his eye, the minister then turned to Jamie and said, "You may now kiss your bride." At that moment, my veil was lifted, and Jamie leaned in for that much anticipated first bridal kiss. From that moment, I surrendered my old name and became united with my husband, enthusiastically taking on his name.

There is a transfer from the old into the new when we enter into a wedding ceremony. While still under my wedding veil, I was my former self. But the moment the minister pronounced us husband and wife and my veil was lifted, a shift took place in my identity, and I entered into something brand-new and glorious. From that day forward, I became grafted into my husband's family and he was grafted into mine. Our flesh became one through our marriage union. His heritage became mine and vice-versa.

The same occurs when we are united with Christ. We take on the name of Jesus. We take on His kinship to the Father. We become sons and daughters of the Highest. And with our veils lifted once and for all, we radiate and reflect the glory of a bride who is in love and is completely loved by her Bridegroom.

CHAPTER SEVENTEEN

He welcomes us to come into the most holy sanctuary in the heavenly realm—boldly and without hesitation. For he has dedicated a new, life-giving way for us to approach God. For just as the veil was torn in two, Jesus's body was torn open to give us free and fresh access to him.

—Hebrews 10:19-20 TPT

Another veil mentioned in Scripture symbolises something wonderfully new as well. At Jesus's death, the veil of the temple was torn in two (Matthew 27:51, Mark 15:38, Luke 23:45). This veil is symbolic of the old covenant function to separate the Israelites from the direct presence of God. No one could enter the Holy of Holies, which was located behind the veil, except on the Day of Atonement. Even then, only the high priest could enter with a sacrificial blood offering.

When the veil was torn at Jesus's death, this represented the ushering in of a new and glorious covenant. Through His sacrificial death, Jesus tore open the veil of separation from God, offering us direct access to God the Father. This means that Jesus re-established true intimacy and relationship with our Creator. We can now enjoy perpetual abiding with the Father, walking and talking with God 'in the cool of the day' (Genesis 3:8).

This was always God's redemptive plan for mankind—a type of perfect Mount Sinai encounter where we have access to our Father anywhere and at any time. Communion with God is not unique to Moses or even to Adam and Eve when they were still abiding with God in the Garden of Eden. It is supposed to be our normal life experience. Just as my son Joel experienced when Jesus visited him in his sleep, encounters with God should not be surprising. On the contrary, we are designed for our very own Mount Sinai encounters, so we should expect an intimate relationship with our Creator all of the time.

Jesus actually modelled for us what it looks like to be in constant communion with the Father. It was the basis for His life mission. He often retreated from the masses to spend time in the presence of God (Luke 5:16). He stated that He must be about His Father's business (Luke 2:49). He stated numerous times that He only said or did what the Father says or does (John 5:19-20; John 12:49). When Jesus gave His disciples a model of prayer to follow (Matthew 6: 9-13), He also urged them—and us—to emulate the communion Jesus had with His heavenly Father.

> Go into your innermost chamber and be alone with Father God, praying to him in secret. (Matthew 6:6 TPT)

In other words, we are invited to find our own Mount Sinai encounter sanctuary, then spend time there communing, praying, and simply enjoying the presence of our heavenly Father.

While Jamie and I were building a new home on a farm in the Victoria countryside, we discussed creating a prayer trail on the property that would lead to an erected cross on one of the ridges. One day while out walking through our farmland, I asked God where He would like the cross to go.

The day had been utterly still to that moment. But just as I asked God this question, a whirlwind began stirring around me. The wind rushed in out of nowhere, and though it only lasted about twenty seconds, it was quite strong and fierce. It was an awe-inspiring moment. Maybe even just ever so slightly similar to what the Israelites encountered at the base of Mount Sinai when they first saw and heard God coming down from Mount Sinai.

> On the morning of the third day there was thunder and lightning, with a thick cloud over the mountain, and a very loud trumpet blast. Everyone in the camp trembled. Then Moses led the people out of the camp to meet with God, and they stood at the foot of the mountain. Mount Sinai was covered with smoke, because the Lord descended on it in fire. The smoke billowed up from it like smoke from a furnace, and the whole mountain trembled violently. As

the sound of the trumpet grew louder and louder, Moses spoke and the voice of God answered him. (Exodus 19:16-19)

When the whirlwind blowing around me suddenly stopped, God impressed on me to look up toward the ridge bordering the northern boundary of our property. As I did so, I saw that during the blast of wind a tree had fallen against another tree. Where it had wedged itself between the other tree's branches, it looked exactly like a cross. It was as though God had answered my query about where to erect a cross by instead creating for me my very own cross.

From that day forward, my prayer trail took me up to this cross formed during the sudden wind. My family affectionately named the hill on which it stood Cross Hill. Moses went up Mount Sinai to abide in God's presence, waiting on Him to receive the truth and revelation God wanted to impart as well as an impartation of God's glory. Jesus too frequently retreated from the masses to pray to His Father in secret. For me, Cross Hill became my very own secret Mount Sinai encounter sanctuary where I too spent time in God's presence, abiding, waiting, and positioning myself to receive His truth and wisdom for my life and that of my family.

How we came to be moving to this new property is another story that resulted from a series of God-conversations and a subsequent dream God gave me in 2014. At the time, our family had been very content in our current residence, which Jamie and I had designed and built just seven years earlier. We'd named our home *Verily*

House, which means House of Truth, and Jamie and I had envisaged growing old together there. We'd daydreamed of a future where we'd be sitting on our wrap-around porch watching future grandchildren playing in our cottage garden and enjoying the fruits of our hard labour.

We'd also achieved almost complete financial freedom at this home. Life felt safe and secure, and we had no intention of moving. But after months of walking and talking with God, Jamie and I both felt a gentle but ever-persuasive nudge from God to move from our beloved Verily House and trust fully in where God was leading us next.

This pressing from the Lord was solidified through a dream I had in August 2014. In the dream, I was standing at an entrance into a farm, which led down a slope into a beautiful little valley. God stood next to me in the dream, and He simply said these words: "I am giving you this land. It is glorious, and it will take your breath away."

The dream was so vivid that when I woke up the next morning I decided to browse online real-estate listings. To my surprise, I came across a listing for a parcel of land that fit the dream description perfectly. Jamie and I immediately drove out to walk the property. When we reached the entrance to the farm, I was overcome with tears. Where I stood looked exactly as where I'd been standing with God in the previous night's dream. It was as though in the night I'd been transported to that very location.

When I looked at the brochure we received from the realtor, its main captions were 'Glorious!' and 'Breath-taking!' These were the very same words God had used to describe the land to me in the dream. I knew then that God was calling us to purchase this property and name it according to the name God had given me some months prior for our future new home: Glorieux. Pronounced "Glory You", Glorieux is a French word that means glorious.

It wasn't immediate, but as Jamie and I abided and communed regularly with God on this subject, our hearts eventually surrendered to the call to leave behind the security of our beloved Verily House and venture out into unchartered terrain. One thing I have come to see through years of faith journeys, if God calls you out of the boat, as He did Peter, He will also prepare you to walk on water. That said, following God's lead doesn't mean things will always be easy or without trouble.

It certainly wasn't without worry for Peter when he walked on water (Matthew 14:27-33). It wasn't trouble-free for the Israelites when God called them out of Egyptian slavery. They'd expected to enter the Promised Land immediately. Instead, they wandered the wilderness for forty years, learning many lessons on their way to the land they'd been promised (Joshua 5:6).

It also wasn't straight-forward for Abraham when God asked him to leave the security of his homeland with only a promise of God's faithfulness and without knowing where God was taking him (Hebrews 11:8-19). Ruth and her mother-in-law Naomi also experienced much hardship when they sought solace and redemption in Naomi's birthplace of Bethlehem (Ruth 1-4). Faith journeys are such because faith requires trust and hope in that which is unseen (Hebrews 11:1).

Our time at Glorieux was no exception. In fact, the lessons we learned on this farm, which I will share in the next chapter, required an even greater measure of intimate union with the Father. This was the reason behind my need to journey up Cross Hill on a daily basis in the first place—to receive God's imparted truth to help our family through our time of need.

CHAPTER EIGHTEEN

When Jesus Christ is unveiled, a greater measure of grace will be released to you.

—1 Peter 1:13 TPT

God positioned us at Glorieux for a reason. Contrary to our original thought, the land He gave us wasn't just a gift. In fact, it became a financial burden. Because of that, I began doubting my ability to hear from God. I even questioned the vivid dream I'd received that had placed us on that property in the first place.

I couldn't fathom why God would have us move from Verily House, a place where we were settled and enjoying financial freedom, to a place that had become a burden and financial liability. But as I journeyed up Cross Hill looking for answers from my Papa, I kept hearing the Spirit of God remind me to trust Him in greater measure rather than leaning 'on [my] own understanding' (Proverbs 3:5-6). The prophet Isaiah's words were also a daily reminder.

> "For my thoughts are not your thoughts, neither are your ways my ways," declares the Lord. "As the heavens are higher than the earth, so are my ways higher than your ways and my thoughts than your thoughts." (Isaiah 55:8-9)

For over a year, God reminded me of this Scripture, asking me to abide and wait on Him for His instructions. This was not easy for me. In the natural, we were struggling financially. It seemed more sensible to finish the build, then sell our property for a small profit and start again elsewhere. But God's ways are not our ways as Isaiah's words resounded over and again in my head. When God asks us to wait, there is usually a very good reason for it.

This certainly proved true one year later. If we'd gone against God's will for us to wait and not move until He instructed us, we would have missed out on receiving a miraculous blessing. We would have compromised the greater measure of God's grace that He wanted to lavish upon us. And we would have missed out on growing our faith to a higher level. You see, faith journeys are always an opportunity for growth as James reminds us in his New Testament epistle.

> When it seems as though you are facing nothing but difficulties, see it as an invaluable opportunity to experience

> the greatest joy that you can! For you know that when your faith is tested it stirs up in you the power of endurance. And then as your endurance grows even stronger, it will release perfection into every part of your being until there is nothing missing and nothing lacking. (James 1:2-4 TPT)

At times the future can seem bleak and uncertain. It certainly felt that way for us back on our Glorieux farm. But God knows and cares about every intricate detail of our lives. He doesn't take us on a faith journey to then leave us stranded along the way. Our heavenly Father 'knows the plans He has for us, plans that are for good and not for disaster, to give us a future and a hope' (Jeremiah 29:11, author's paraphrase).

We often see things from a present-day perspective only. But God sees past, present, and future in perfect clarity. In our case, this included a property boom we didn't see on the horizon that doubled the value of our Glorieux farm in just one year. Talk about God's greater measure of His providential grace!

We came to realise that moving to Glorieux had just been a steppingstone for what God was releasing into our lives. It was the shift needed to get us out of our comfort zone at Verily House and into trusting in God's plans in greater measure. King Solomon reminds:

> Many are the plans in a person's heart, but it is the Lord's purpose that prevails. (Proverbs 19:21)

The plans we have are not always God's perfect plan for our future. Jamie and I had made plans to move our family to Glorieux and make our home there permanently. When that didn't work out as we'd planned, our next thought was to sell Glorieux as quickly as possible and count our losses. Thank goodness God's plans are so much better than our own and His purposes always prevail.

Through our abiding close and waiting on the Holy Spirit's direction, God abundantly provided for us. He enabled us to purchase another property just up the road, a pine plantation we had always admired and loved. Due to selling Glorieux at the perfect time, Jamie could afford to have his first sabbatical since beginning his work career almost thirty-five years earlier, and because of God's providence we both could pursue more ministry.

It's not always easy to patiently wait for God to direct our paths. But His ways are higher than ours, and they are well worth the wait!

Our heavenly Father wants to unveil more of His glory to His beloved. He longs to meet each one of us on our very own Mount Sinai encounter sanctuary, wherever or whatever that looks like for each of us. We have a loving Father who desires to impart His truths and pearls of wisdom to all His children.

In fact, Proverbs 1:20 tells us that Wisdom 'cries out in the street' desperate to be heard (author's paraphrase). This means that the Spirit of God wants to commune with us. He longs for us to have our very own 'in the cool of the day' walks and talks with Him. Our daily 'cuppa with our Papa'. Our Cross Hill encounter sanctuary experiences.

This is the Father's heart for His children.

For me, whether walking up to Cross Hill until we moved again in 2018 or along country lanes as is more typical for me these days, walking and talking with God is paramount for my hearing, knowing, and then following the voice of God. These are my Mount Sinai encounter sanctuaries. The secret chamber Jesus instructs us to go into to pray. These will be different for each of us. But regardless of location, spending time in intimate communion with God on a daily basis is a non-negotiable for me. It is the better Mary posture of *abiding* as we discussed in Mary of Bethany's story in earlier chapters.

There is no bias or discrimination when it comes to spending time with our Creator God. My son's night visit with Jesus proved this true. As God's children and through our union with His Son, we each host the presence of His Spirit. This means we can all enter into our very own Mount Sinai encounter sanctuaries anywhere at any time and on an even greater measure through our relationship with Christ.

Jesus is waiting for us to come and abide at His feet and receive from Him. God's Holy Spirit yearns to impart His truth and wisdom to His beloved. We have been invited to commune daily with our Father in heaven. As we contemplate His glory with unveiled faces, God offers us a greater and greater measure of His transformational love and glory—if only we will choose to receive it!

MARY POSTURE

Abide, Wait, and Receive

LESSON # 7: We host the presence of God through our union with His Son Jesus. This means His Spirit dwells within us, therefore with unveiled faces we can receive more of His transformational glory. Will you choose to enter your very own Mount Sinai encounter sanctuary today? Will you choose to abide and wait on God, whatever and wherever that looks like for you? Our heavenly Father longs for you to come and spend time in His presence. It is out of that close union with God that you will receive a greater measure of His grace outpouring and that He will impart to you a greater portion of His divine wisdom and revelation.

New Bridal Dance

Dance, dance, dear Shulamite, Angel-Princess! Dance, and we'll feast our eyes on your grace! Everyone wants to see the Shulamite dance her victory dances of love and peace.
—Song of Songs 6:13 MSG

LYRICS OF MY HEART

O Love Divine, How Sweet Thou Art

Forever would I take my seat
With Mary at the Master's feet!
Be this my happy choice;
My only care, delight, and bliss,
My joy, my heaven on earth be this,
To hear the Bridegroom's voice.

—By Charles Wesley

CHAPTER NINETEEN

Dance Of Intimacy

Then young women will dance and be glad, young men and old as well.

—Jeremiah 31:13

In mid-December 2020, I was facilitating a House of Prayer worship service in Daylesford, a beautiful tourist town renowned for its natural mineral springs that is located over 100 kilometres from Victoria's capital city, Melbourne. At this service, I had a vision of a bridal dance between Jesus and His bride, the Church. Immediately I heard the Lord say these words:

"I am leading My bride into a new bridal dance. If My people let Me take the lead as your Bridegroom, I will teach you this new bridal dance so that when the time comes to showcase it to the world, we will be completely in-sync, reconciled to one another, ready, and confident in the dance as a bride and Bridegroom. But if My bride tries to take the lead, she will fall into the same moves as she's always done before. If she doesn't follow My lead, My bride will be out of beat with the Father's rhythm and out of sync with those who have already learned this new bridal dance."

To me, this is a beautiful vision of Jesus's deep desire for His bride to come into an intimate union with Him and to trust Him implicitly with the leading of His Church. Just as the prophet Jeremiah described the young men and women of Israel dancing with joy over God's redemption and deliverance in this chapter's opening verse (see Jeremiah 31:1-14), so our Bridegroom's heart right now is for His beloved to walk (or dance!) and talk with Him in the cool of our day (Genesis 3:8).

In other words, Jesus is inviting us to enjoy true intimacy with our Bridegroom as the bride of Christ so we can position ourselves to hear His voice more clearly, thereby knowing and following Jesus's lead as co-heirs with Him to the kingdom of heaven (Romans 8:17). Through that intimate union with Jesus, we can step further into owning our true identity and indeed take up our rightful position as His partner to see the Father's will done here on earth as it is in heaven as Jesus prayed in the model prayer He gave His disciples.

> Your kingdom come, your will be done, on earth as it is in heaven. (Matthew 6:10)

The three Mary postures of abiding, waiting, and receiving, each point to an intimate union we can enjoy with Jesus. By applying these, we can learn to be in-step with this new bridal dance, which is simply an image of being in time and in-sync with Jesus's every move. As I've said numerous times before, true intimacy with God is actually part of our original design. We are created for relationship with our Creator. Walking and talking with God in the cool of our day is a description of friendship and communion that is part of our heritage.

As discussed in the previous section, talking with God face-to-face as Moses did is available to all of us but on an even greater measure through our union with Christ. When we abide in Jesus and feed off His Word, when we get to know Him personally and intimately, waiting on His direction for our lives, we will then be positioned to receive more of His glory and indeed be ready to move as He leads us.

Scripture reveals that Jesus is returning for His bride. So it makes sense that He is inviting us into a deeper relationship before His return. After all, what bridegroom would want to come back for a bride who knows of him but hasn't already invested time in knowing him intimately? Jesus wants to be known personally and on a greater level just as our Bridegroom knows every intricate detail of His most beloved right down to the number of hairs on our head (Luke 12:7). The apostle Paul describes what our relationship with the Son of God should look like through the example of the marriage union.

> Marriage is the beautiful design of the Almighty, a great mystery of Christ and his church. (Ephesians 5:32 TPT)

Marriage is the highest form of an intimate union. When we accept Jesus as our Lord and Saviour, we become part of the bride of Christ, united with Him in partnership similar to that of a marriage. Our Bridegroom wants His Church to replicate the marriage union. He wants us to get to know Him experientially, intimately, and with partnership in mind. He is seeking those who desire to ignite a passion for their 'first love,' Jesus (Revelation 2:4, NKJV). Or reignite for those who need to 'fan the flame' (2 Timothy 1:6).

This partnership we enter into is an eternal one. When Jesus returns, we will rule and reign alongside our Bridegroom.

> You have made them to be a kingdom and priests to serve our God, and they will reign on the earth. (Revelation 5:10)

And it begins with having an intimate, knowing relationship with our Bridegroom now, a bond that parallels that of a betrothed couple who are completely enamoured with one another. Back in January 1995 when I was just eighteen years of age, Jamie was staying with my family. One morning about 3 a.m., he awoke me to go on a romantic outing to Byron Bay, a New South Wales beachside town located about two hours south of my parents' home in Queensland. Thankfully, I'm a morning person, as I mentioned in my introduction, so this very early wake-up call was an adventure on which I was excited to join Jamie.

Once we arrived in Byron Bay, Jamie and I made our

way along a beach located on the most easterly point of Australia to watch the sunrise. It was 5:20 a.m. I know the exact minute because I wanted to remember this day for the rest of my life so I looked at my watch to solidify that moment in time.

As the sun rose over the ocean, Jamie bent on one knee and proposed to me. Immediately as if on cue, a dolphin jumped out of the water to join in our celebrations. Jamie's proposal was everything my young, fantastical self ever hoped and dreamed it would be.

For the next eight months of our betrothal, I retold our engagement story to anyone and everyone who would listen. I showed off my sparkly new diamond engagement ring. I couldn't stop thinking about my soon-to-be husband and my upcoming dream wedding day. It was all-consuming. Emotionally and intimately, I was invested in my relationship with Jamie.

This engagement period and even the courting years are some of the most heightened experiences of burning passion a couple will ever experience. The anticipation of marrying your one-and-only is captivating. When a bride walks down the aisle, her eyes are fixed firmly on her bridegroom. His eyes are locked fervently on his bride. At that moment, nothing else matters. It's just the two of them.

Many of us who are married can reminisce and retell over and again how we met our spouses. We can probably detail what the proposal was like and the intricate details of our wedding day. Even those not yet married often imagine this day. I know my daughter Faith dreams of what is to come with the enthusiasm of one who has actually experienced it.

This type of excitement we have for our earthly relationships, particularly in those early days, is exactly what our Bridegroom Jesus is longing and yearning for when it comes to an intimate embrace with His bride. Our passion for Jesus is to mirror that first all-consuming love of a marriage union. We are called to:

> Love the Lord our God with all our heart, and with all our soul and with all our mind. (Matthew 22:37)

This is an all-consuming love into which our Bridegroom invites us, an ardent passion for His bride we can't even come close to reciprocating. God wants all of us because He wants to show us how to love and be completely loved in return. Our earthly relationships can become strained and even break down. But the love Jesus offers can never be weakened. Nothing in our present or future circumstances can separate us from the passionate love God has for us as the apostle Paul wrote in his letter to the church in Rome.

> So now I live with the confidence that there is nothing in the universe with the power to separate us from God's love . . . There is no power above us or beneath us—no power that could ever be found in the universe that can distance us from God's passionate love, which is lavished upon us through our Lord Jesus, the Anointed One!
> (Romans 8:38-39 TPT)

This means that the love on offer to us from our Bridegroom is beyond our wildest imagination, as Paul also described.

> Deeply intimate and far-reaching. How enduring and inclusive it is! Endless love beyond measurement that transcends our understanding—this extravagant love pours into you until you are filled to overflowing with the fullness of God! (Ephesians 3:18-19 TPT)

This love offered to us as the bride of Christ is perfect and beyond our earthly comprehension. John 15:13 says that the greatest love of all is to lay down one's life for another. Our Bridegroom did just that when He went to the cross for every one of us.

Partnership is also a vital element of a good marriage union. In fact, when God first created mankind, God made woman as a complementary partner to man.

> Now the Lord God said, "It is not good [beneficial] for the man to be alone; I will make him a helper [one who balances him – a counterpart who is] suitable and complementary for him." (Genesis 2:18 AMP)

Part of this new bridal dance of intimacy is knowing and understanding our partnership role as the bride of Christ. We are urged to take up our rightful authority as co-heirs to the kingdom of heaven. In fact, our Bridegroom has given us His very own set of kingdom keys so we can partner with Him to bring more of heaven to earth.

> I will give you the keys of the kingdom of heaven; whatever you bind on earth will be bound in heaven, and whatever you loose on earth will be loosed in heaven.
> (Matthew 16:19)

The prophet Isaiah prophesied that the Messiah would come and proclaim the good news to the poor, bind up the broken-hearted, proclaim freedom for the captives, release prisoners from darkness, proclaim the year of the Lord's favour, comfort all who mourn, and heal the sick and the lame (Isaiah 53 and 61). Jesus fulfilled these prophesies through the countless miracles He performed, and He promises that His bride will do the same mighty miracles and even greater miracles.

> I tell you this timeless truth: The person who follows me in faith, believing in me, will do the same mighty miracles that I do—even greater miracles than these because I go to be with my Father! (John 14:12 TPT)

This 'timeless truth' is part of our destiny. Signs and wonders are for now as much as they were in Jesus's day and even in the first-century church. God validated the early church's ministry with 'signs, astonishing wonders, all kinds of powerful miracles, and by the gifts of the Holy Spirit, which he distributed as he desired' (Hebrews 2:4, TPT). He validates our ministry today with signs, wonders, and gifts as well for we are all one in Christ Jesus (Romans 12:5). Since Jesus is the same yesterday, today, and forever (Hebrews 13:8), we partake of the same gifts that were bestowed upon those who have gone before us.

Jesus said that the harvest is plentiful but the workers are few (Matthew 9:37). This means it's all hands on deck. Every person in the body of Christ has been purposed for such a time as now. We all have unique assignments handed to us by our Creator, and no member of the body of Christ is of less value than another.

In fact, the gifts with which we've been endowed are unique and creative only to the body of Christ. They are designed to complement Christ's Church in perfect partnership and to equip His people for works of service. In other words, our differences shouldn't be a divisive point of contention but are actually our greatest strength. They enable us to serve one another as well as to be a light to the world.

For this reason, I'd like to focus next on the bridal dance of unison. If we are to partner and complement one another through our different gifts as well as prepare for our Bridegroom's return, the bride of Christ needs to be ready for what comes next as well as dancing in perfect unison as one body of believers and with Jesus leading the dance.

CHAPTER TWENTY

Dance Of Unison

My Father's house has many rooms; if that were not so, would I have told you that I am going there to prepare a place for you? And if I go and prepare a place for you, I will come back and take you to be with me that you also may be where I am.

—John 14:2-3

Greater miracles than Jesus performed is part of our commission. But it is only made possible out of an intimate embrace with our Bridegroom. Jesus desires to lead the bridal dance. He invites us to abide close to Him, wait on His wise instruction, and move only when we receive His authority to do so. This was actually something God offered the Israelites while they were wandering in the wilderness. They too had to learn to *abide, wait,* and *receive,* and they did this in unison as one nation.

God had placed a pillar of cloud over the Israelite camp by day and a pillar of fire over them by night (Exodus 13:21-22). By abiding under this cloud or fire, they received God's protection and provision. When God's glory cloud moved, the whole Israelite nation packed up and set out to follow the cloud. Wherever the cloud settled, the Israelites encamped and waited for their next set of instructions (Numbers 9:17).

The Israelites knew that to follow God's glory cloud was the better option. It would provide them with the security they needed as a nation while out in the wilderness. They also knew it would ultimately lead them to the Promised Land.

The same principle applies to us. When we allow Jesus to lead the way, when we move only at His command by following His glory cloud, we will be in sync with the new bridal dance. Which means we will be in total unison as one body of believers with the Father's will.

Part of this bridal dance is making ourselves ready for our Bridegroom's return. Revelation 19:7 tells us that by the time the wedding feast of Jesus and His bride has come, the bride of Christ will have 'made herself ready'. The passage doesn't give any indication of precisely how we have made ourselves ready. But Scripture does point to our need to be prepared, watch for the signs, and have our lamps lit brightly in readiness for our Bridegroom's return.

In Jewish culture at the time of Christ, the bridegroom was responsible for preparing a home for his bride before the wedding ceremony. During this time period, the bride would remain with her parents and be in preparation mode. When the day of the wedding finally arrived, the bride was responsible to prepare herself for the wedding banquet, then remain on watch for her bridegroom who could arrive at any time and without any notice.

Based on this tradition, Jesus shared a parable of a wedding feast to urge His bride to be prepared, get ready, and wait for His return (Matthew 25:1-13). In the parable, ten maidens were invited to the wedding banquet, but only five were prepared for the bridegroom's arrival with lit lamps and plenty of oil in case there was any delay.

The other five maidens allowed their lamps to run low with no oil to refill them. They had to run to the store to purchase more oil. While they were gone, the bridegroom arrived and took those maidens who were ready with him into the wedding banquet. By the time the unprepared maidens returned, the doors into the banquet location were already closed so they were refused entrance.

The point of this parable is for us to get prepared. Jesus wants our lamps lit brightly. He wants us to be like the five prepared maidens who had plenty of oil. Oil is often represented in Scripture as symbolic of the overflow of Holy Spirit. The surplus of oil these five prepared maidens had ready represents an increased anointing of the Holy Spirit on the bride of Christ.

After Jesus received water baptism and the Holy Spirit rested upon Him, He began a ministry marked by miraculous signs and wonders (Acts 10:38). This parable of the ten maidens shows us that the bride of Christ will be overflowing with the anointing of God's Spirit in the last days. The same power that rested on Jesus will rest on our shoulders as well, and the greater miracles our Bridegroom has promised will follow our ministries.

The five prepared maidens were also eagerly anticipating their bridegroom's arrival. Matthew 24 says that the last days will be like the days of Noah where people just went on living their normal lives eating, drinking, marrying, and having children until the flood came. They didn't realise the end was near until Noah entered the ark, and then it was too late.

In contrast, Scripture tells us that the bride of Christ will be ready. This is a definite statement. When we abide and wait on Jesus, we will be so in-sync with our Bridegroom's every move that we will know the signs foretelling that Jesus is nigh. This means we will also be ready and waiting with eager anticipation to receive our Bridegroom at His return.

When I was pregnant with my three children, I prepared well for each of their arrivals. During the last trimester of each pregnancy, I really got into what is termed a 'nesting syndrome'. If you don't know about the nesting syndrome, believe me it's a real thing!

In summary, it is an overwhelming urge to clean and organise everything to get one's home ready for the new baby's arrival. In my case, everything got pulled out of cupboards for a clean-down. My house sparkled with cleanliness. I had my travel bag sorted and packed early in the last trimester.

And of course I knew the birthing signs to look out for. I still didn't know the precise day or hour in which I would deliver my child, but that didn't matter because I was ready and my house was in order. All I had to do was wait for the day of my baby's birth.

Like a bridegroom in Jesus's day who returned to his family home to prepare a place for his bride, Jesus is preparing a place for us in our heavenly Father's house (John 14:3). By traditional Jewish wedding custom, the father of the bride would advise his future son-in-law when he was to return for his bride. Likewise, Jesus will only come back for His bride at the hour appointed by our heavenly Father.

In the meantime, we need to prepare ourselves to be ready and waiting for His return because we don't know the hour or the day of His arrival (Luke 12:40), just the signs to look out for (Matthew 24). This means we need to have a type of 'nesting syndrome' so that no matter when Jesus returns, we will have our house in order and our bags packed ready to go.

There is a great harvest of souls still to come into the kingdom of God. Many have yet to learn of the wedding banquet our Bridegroom is preparing on our behalf (Matthew 22, Revelation 19). In many cultures, the parents of the bride traditionally send out wedding invitations prior to their daughter's wedding date. In recent years, a 'save the date' notice has also become popular to send out prior to the actual invitation being delivered.

Similarly, the bride of Christ has been commissioned by our heavenly Father to send out invitations to our wedding feast on His behalf. In other words, we have been commissioned to preach the good news message of Jesus to the ends of the world so that everyone receives an opportunity to accept the wedding invitation and become part of God's family (Matthew 28:19-20).

I said earlier that it is all hands on deck for the final preparations before Jesus returns. The beauty of the bride of Christ is that we are all different. We've each been endowed with grace-gifts that complement the body of Christ. These gifts come in great variety and are to be used to edify, encourage, and strengthen the Church.

> God has carefully designed each member and placed it in the body to function as he desires. Diversity is required, for if the body consisted of one single part, there wouldn't be a body at all! So now we see that there are many differing parts and functions, but one body. You are the body of the Anointed One [Jesus], and each of you is a unique and a vital part of it. (1 Corinthians 12:18-20, 27-28 TPT)

> In the human body there are many parts and organs, each with a unique function. And so it is in the body of Christ. For though we are many, we've all been mingled into one body in Christ. This means that we are all vitally joined to one another, with each contributing to the others. (Romans 12:4-5 TPT)

Unity in our diversity is essential for the season we are in. I recently had a follow-on vision of the bridal dance I described at the beginning of this section. The first

Dance of Unison

vision focused on Jesus and our need to follow His lead, to be in-sync with His every move, because He is central to everything we do. This new vision focused on the bride of Christ made up of millions of believers dancing in perfect harmony and unison.

In the vision, we each held a brightly-lit lamp like the five maidens mentioned in the wedding parable. The moves we were dancing to looked like a tidal wave of symmetry and motion. Though many, we were completely in-sync and in one accord with the Father's rhythm as each of us followed the lead of our Bridegroom. We were like an enormous choir singing many different parts that come together in glorious harmony.

I truly believe Jesus is calling the bride of Christ to unity even in our differences. First and foremost, He is calling for our reconciliation back to Himself, a return to our first love mentioned earlier (Revelation 2:4). Secondly, He is calling for our reconciliation with each other. We are better together because there is strength in numbers. The Church needs to stand united as one. King Solomon wisely wrote of the importance of togetherness in his book of Ecclesiastes.

> Two people are better off than one, for they can help each other succeed. If one person falls, the other can reach out and help. But someone who falls alone is in real trouble. A person standing alone can be attacked and defeated, but two can stand back-to-back and conquer. Three are even better, for a triple-braided cord is not easily broken. (Ecclesiastes 4:9-10,12 NLT)

This picture of togetherness shows us how important it is to have each other's back. The bride of Christ does not need to look or act all the same to be in unison. The Church is made up of different parts for a reason—to make us whole. When we are in accordance with God's Word, we complement and strengthen each other despite our unique differences. This makes us a formidable force and is something that should be celebrated.

While writing this book, I had a collection of dreams on the same night that all point to the importance of unity in our differences. The first dream was a simple vision of a stack of multi-coloured glass cups that were all different but complemented each other beautifully. The second dream was simply a Scripture from the apostle Paul's epistle to the Galatian church.

> There is neither Jew nor Gentle, neither slave nor free, nor
> is there male and female, for you are all one in Christ Jesus.
> (Galatians 3:28)

In the third dream, I was coming in last in a 400-meter hurdle race. At the halfway mark, I decided to turn around and run back the same way I'd come. People were calling out that I was going the wrong way. Others were saying what I was doing wasn't fair. Still others were saying this isn't the way we do things. Then the race officials announced that I had still run the same distance, so it didn't really matter how I got to the end as long as I finished the race.

As the bride of Christ, we are all one body but have different functions operating out of our different giftings according to the grace given to us (Romans 12:6). God is calling for unity in our differences. He is asking us to stand in one accord, and dance in unison. Such a tidal wave of unison will have an amazing ripple effect across our globe and might just usher in the great harvest that has been prophesied (Luke 10:2).

Many more invitations to the wedding feast between Jesus and His bride still need to be sent out because God wants all to be saved (1 Timothy 2:4). Through our unique gifts, we can each partner with our Bridegroom in sending out these invitations in our own special way.

There is also a greater measure of intimacy into which we are invited in readiness for Jesus's return. He wants to be our treasure. Just as Jesus lavishes us extravagantly with love and devotion, so too He wants to be the object of our extravagant love and worship. This is something for which Mary of Bethany was renowned and which we will look at next.

CHAPTER TWENTY-ONE

> Do you see this woman kneeling here? She is doing for me what you didn't bother to do . . . This is why she has shown me such extravagant love.
>
> —Luke 7:44, 47 TPT

Each of the four gospels includes an account of a woman who extravagantly poured out a very expensive jar of perfume to anoint Jesus (Matthew 26:6-13; Mark 14:1-9; Luke 7:36-50; John 12:1-8). In each account, Jesus was being hosted at a feast. Three accounts give the location as Bethany (Matthew 26:6-13; Mark 14:1-9; John 12:1-8). Three of the accounts mention the host being a man named Simon (Matthew 26:6-13; Mark 14:1-9; Luke 7:36-50), two of them specifying Simon the leper, the third mentioning Simon the Pharisee.

The fourth account (John 12:1-8) is the only one that names the woman involved as Mary, sister of Martha and Lazarus (see also John 11:2). Many scholars believe the various accounts are describing at least two separate occasions with at least two different women. I don't have the definitive answer one way or another. But for the purpose of this illustration on extravagant love, I will take another popular stance and suggest that at least two of these gospel accounts, in Luke and John, are speaking of the same dinner party involving the one woman actually named, Mary of Bethany.

Regardless of whether or not it is a single dinner party or woman, these accounts show us an incredibly intimate devotion to Jesus through an extravagant act of love. Something to which I believe Jesus is calling us and certainly something Mary of Bethany was highly esteemed for.

In Luke's account, the woman at the dinner party (we are going to assume this is Mary of Bethany as named in John 12) learned that Jesus was having dinner at the home of a Jewish religious leader by the name of Simon. She may have known this through her sister Martha since the John 12 account says that Martha was serving this meal while their brother Lazarus was one of the dinner guests. Taking an alabaster jar filled with an expensive perfume called nard (John 12:3), Mary entered Simon's home and went straight to Jesus.

Just a little cultural note here, three of the passages mention that Jesus is reclining at the table (Matthew 26:6-13; Mark 14:1-9; John 12:1-8) while the Luke passage describes Mary as standing behind Jesus at His feet. This is because guests ate stretched out on cushions or rugs around a low table or even a serving cloth spread on the floor. So the feet of Jesus would have been stretched out away from the table as Mary came up behind Him.

Without caring who was watching her, Mary knelt at Jesus's feet, broken and weeping, her tears falling onto Jesus's feet. As she cried, she dried His feet with her long hair and kissed them over and over. Then she opened her flask and anointed His feet with her costly perfume as an act of extravagant love and devotion.

In three accounts, this act is immediately criticised by the disciples and others around for this open display of what was seen as wasteful worship (John 12:4-6). In each, Jesus reprimanded her critics. But in Luke's account, the host Simon inwardly sneers that such a sinful woman is touching Jesus, which Jesus should know if He were really a prophet.

Jesus could clearly read Simon's thoughts because He rebuked Simon, saying:

> Do you see this woman kneeling here? She is doing for me what you didn't bother to do. When I entered your home as your guest, you didn't think about offering me water to wash the dust off my feet. Yet she came into your home and washed my feet with her many tears and then dried my feet with her hair. You didn't even welcome me into your home with the customary kiss of greeting, but from the moment I came in, she has not stopped kissing my feet. You didn't take the time to anoint my head with fragrant oil, but she anointed my head and feet with the finest perfume. She has been forgiven of all her many sins. This is why she has

shown me such extravagant love. But those who assume they have very little to be forgiven will love me very little. (Luke 7:44-47 TPT)

Because Mary had been forgiven much, she could not help but pour out her extravagant love in return. She no longer treasured the expensive jar of perfume because her treasure was now found in Jesus. He had captured her whole heart. Since she was now a woman who knew she was deeply loved and who was also deeply in love with her Bridegroom, this made her want to lavish Jesus with her extravagant love and devotion.

I mentioned earlier that Jesus wants to come back for a bride who knows Him intimately and experientially, who receives and reciprocates His extravagant love as Mary of Bethany did. In modern cultures except where arranged marriages still take place, a couple expects to get to be well acquainted before the marriage celebration takes place. There is courtship involved, which includes a getting to know one another period.

It would be unusual these days to enter into a marriage having only received someone's bio. Such might give us basic information about who we are marrying. But there is so much more to experience and discover through an actual experiential one-on-one relationship with our fiancé. The same goes for our union with Jesus. Jesus is the Word of God as the Gospel of John makes clear:

In the beginning was the Word and the Word was with God, and the Word was God. (John 1:1)

We experience Jesus through reading His living, breathing Word. That is His bio for us. It is the foundation of our faith. If you want a place to start with intimacy with God, sinking into His written Word is the first and best place to start. But along with reading God's Word, we are also called to experience intimacy through our communion with the Word who has a name—Jesus.

Intimacy with God is connected to our destiny. When we accept Jesus as our Saviour, our lives begin the transformational process as we also looked at earlier. The more connected we are to our Bridegroom, the more we will be reshaped into His likeness and operate out of our true authority as sons and daughters of God. This means that part of our metamorphosis from our old self into Christ's likeness will include some shedding of the deadwood we carry in our lives that need to be pruned by God the Father as Jesus described.

> I am the true vine, and my Father is the gardener. He cuts off every branch in me that bears no fruit, while every branch that does bear fruit he prunes so that it will be even more fruitful. (John 15:1-2)

Early in 2020, God began a new pruning in me. A prophetic word that many leading prophets had declared at the turn of the decade came from Hebrews 12:27, which speaks of 'everything that can be shaken will be shaken!'

This certainly proved true for me in 2020 as the walls of my own foundation were shaken and God began pruning away the deadwood in my own life in what can be termed my 'God-makeover'.

Jeremiah 18:4 gives us an image of a potter who took a freshly moulded clay pot that had been marred, then crushed, squeezed, and shaped it into another vessel that was to his liking. I too was in a renovation of sorts with God pulling me apart, remoulding me, and thereby realigning my destiny.

What this experience taught me is that when we pursue a greater level of intimacy with our Bridegroom, we may require a God-makeover. As Jesus said in another parable, you can't put new wine into old wineskins (Matthew 9:14-17, Mark 2:18-22, Luke 5:33-39). For me to step into a greater measure of intimacy with God as I desired, God first needed to tear down some of the walls I had put up over the years. The facades of my ego that were getting in the way of true intimacy with my Bridegroom needed to fall. The veil of deception around my identity needed to be lifted so I could draw closer to Him, unveiled and ready for the more.

God wants a greater measure of freedom for each one of us. He wants to break down whatever barrier holds us back from drawing closer to Him so that we can walk out our true destiny in fullness and in freedom. Sometimes that requires God pruning the deadwood in our lives that isn't producing good fruit.

Ephesians 5:27 tells us that everything Christ does and says is designed to bring the best out of His bride, who will be glorious and radiant, beautiful and holy, without fault and flaw at His return. This means we can expect change that will transfigure us into Christ's very own gloriously beautiful and holy image. In other words, we can expect our very own caterpillar-to-butterfly metamorphous.

I liken this to a married couple who have been married for a very long time. You will see such an older couple finish each other's sentences. They will sometimes talk on behalf of their spouse. They know what each other wants before it's even been asked. They will even take on each other's mannerisms. It's as though they've become a mirror image of each other.

This is the type of intimate connection that Ephesians 5:31-32 says is a vivid example of the marriage union between Christ and His bride. When we commune frequently with our Bridegroom, when we spend much time abiding in His presence and waiting on Him, we will then receive and reflect more of His glory. Jesus said of His close union with the Father:

> Whatever I say is just what the Father has told me to say. (John 12:49)

We should be able to say the same thing if we are experiencing close intimacy with God's Spirit. After all, Jesus tells us that:

> If we abide in him and his words abide in us we can ask whatever we wish and it will be done. (John 15:7-8 NKJV)

A close union with our Bridegroom means we know His heart as well as His will. We will therefore confidently partner with our Father's will on earth as it is in heaven (Matthew 6:10). I truly believe that now is the time to ignite or reignite our first love for Jesus. We are invited to be extravagantly loved and to extravagantly love our Bridegroom in return.

It is also time to announce our engagement and upcoming wedding to the world. There are many guests still to be invited, and we have the privilege to speak of God's goodness, describe His amazing love, recount His mercy, and share the wonders of His miraculous power.

It is time we draw closer to Jesus and embrace His invitation into a greater depth of intimacy than ever before. We should desire more than anything the same yearning as the apostle Paul had when he wrote to the Church in Philippi:

> I continually long to know the wonders of Jesus more fully.
> I want to know him inside and out! (Philippians 3:10 TPT, author's paraphrase)

The date for our wedding feast has been set by our heavenly Father. It is more lavish and extravagant than our eyes have ever beheld. Our invitations have already been sent out, and if you have accepted Jesus as your Saviour, there is a place card with your name on it seated right next to our Beloved.

Not only are we guests at this wedding feast but the guests of honour. Jesus has prepared a Bridegroom's speech full of His abundant love for His perfect bride. In fact, it echoes King Solomon's intimate words:

Extravagant Love

> You are my beloved and I am yours. (Song of Solomon 6:3)

The Father too is beaming with pride for His Son's wife. She has become as much a child of His as His Son ever was (Ephesians 1:5-6). As for the bride, we are dressed in our pure white linen, a gift that cost our Bridegroom everything even unto death (Revelation 19:8).

As we walk down the aisle, we are covered in His grace and mercy, wrapped in His forgiveness and love, with a bridal gown made of His pure, holy righteousness. Our eyes are fixed firmly on Jesus, the Author and Perfecter of our faith (Hebrews 12:2). Out of us radiates the beauty that is reflected in our Beloved. As we take our place on the dance floor, ready to showcase our bridal dance in perfect unison together with our Bridegroom, we hear the angels cry out the wonderful anthem:

> Hallelujah! For our Lord God Almighty reigns! Let us rejoice and exalt him and give him glory because the wedding celebration of the Lamb has come. And his bride has made herself ready! (Revelation 19:7)

MARY POSTURE

Abide, Wait, and Receive

LESSON # 8: Jesus wants to lead us in a new bridal dance. Will you choose to abide ever so closely in an intimate embrace with your Saviour today? Will you ready yourself, eagerly waiting for His return? Will you receive His far-reaching, extravagant love that He longs to lavish upon you while reciprocating that all-consuming love in return?

Beginning to End

I am the Alpha and the Omega, the First and the Last, the Beginning and the End.
—Revelation 22:13

PRAYER OF MY HEART

Set Your Watch Over Me

Lord, set Your watch over me today.
Fix Your gaze upon Your child.
Let my feet never stumble,
Nor my mind become troubled,
But let my soul be under Your care.

Lord, set Your watch over me today.
Place my life on firm foundation.
Direct my times and seasons.
The whole world is in Your palms,
So light up my path, and lead the way.

Lord, set Your watch over me today.
Examine my heart, make it pure.
Wash me in Your righteousness.
Lead me out of temptation,
And hide me, God, under Your shadow.

Lord, set Your watch over me today.
You alone know the days and hours.
You see all and know all things.
In Your image we are made,
So behold Your devoted this day.

—By Nicole Zoch

CHAPTER TWENTY-TWO

Family Heirloom

Surely I am with you always, to the very end of [time].
—Matthew 28:20

An aunt who had recently read my first book *Having Faith* shared with me a mysterious event I hadn't known about that took place on the day of my daughter's birth. For Jamie and me, this was a day that marked the end of one era and the beginning of a brand-new season of life. For nine years of longing to be parents, we'd been in a season of abiding and waiting. Once our daughter Faith was born, we moved into a season of receiving the great blessing of answered prayer. The following poetic praise that King David wrote to God expresses this time in our lives.

> Lord, I will exalt you and lift you high, for you have lifted me up on high! O Lord, my healing God, I cried out for a miracle and you healed me! (Psalm 30:1-2 TPT)

My aunt and her family live on the southeast coast of Australia about an hour south of Sydney and some 800 kilometres away from where I was delivering my firstborn. That is where an unusual event related to a family heirloom gave time a whole new meaning to me.

My great-great-grandfather from Austria had made a fob-watch that had been passed down the family line through my dad's mum, my Oma. Since her passing in the late 1980s, the watch had remained at my uncle and aunt's home. The watch had stopped working decades earlier. When my relatives took it to various watch repairers and jewellers, they always received the same response: "It could be cleaned, but the parts are too old to be fixed."

The watch was tucked away somewhere in my aunt and uncle's closet, and they thought nothing more of it for many years. But on the day of Faith's birth, something curious transpired. My aunt and uncle heard a ticking coming from their closet. When they investigated, they discovered that the fob-watch, which hadn't worked for decades, had suddenly begun keeping time again. It continued to function perfectly for the first week of my daughter's life, after which it once again stopped as abruptly as it began. It hasn't worked ever since.

I have no idea why the watch began to tell time again after so many years of not working on the very day of my daughter's birth. But as with her sudden miraculous conception after nine years of waiting, the watch reminds me that God is outside of time. God has the beginning and the end at His disposal. He is without borders or limitations. God's timing is perfect, and it's exactly in alignment with His ultimate will for our lives.

That is because our Father is the God of the miraculous. The woman with the issue of blood was a perfect testament to this. She waited twelve years for her *then one day* moment before being *suddenly* and miraculously healed by Jesus. She may have thought God would never show up. But God always turns up exactly on time even if the outcome is different from our expectations. In this woman's case, Jesus was not late in coming nor did He tarry. He arrived exactly when necessary to showcase God's glory and answer her prayers in spectacular form. His timing was perfect.

All three Marys are a testament to God's perfect timing as well. For Mary of Bethany, this was never more evident than when her brother Lazarus died (John 11). Jesus was away when Lazarus became deathly sick. Mary and her sister Martha had sent word to Jesus to come, believing that if He were present their brother would be made well again.

But though Jesus loved Mary, Martha, and Lazarus very much, He remained where He was for another two days, knowing full well that during that time Lazarus would die. He knew this death would cause pain to His friends. But He also knew that time was in His hands. This was a moment to bring glory and praise to God and reveal the greatness of the Son of God (John 11:4). So Jesus let time pass by because there was an even more perfect time yet to come.

Had Jesus returned home earlier to find Lazarus merely sick, the measure of His greatness would not have been made evident. After all, Jesus had performed many previous healings. The miraculous followed Him wherever He went. But this was an opportunity to reveal another level of His authority as the Son of God. This was the opportune moment for Jesus to be glorified as Jesus Himself made clear.

> [Jesus] replied to them, "Now is the time for the Son of Man to be glorified. Let me make this clear: A single grain of wheat will never be more than a single grain of wheat unless it drops into the ground and dies. Because then it sprouts and produces a great harvest of wheat – all because one grain died". (John 12:23-24 TPT)

When Jesus finally returned, He found His beloved friend had already been entombed for four days. People had come from all over to mourn Lazarus's death. Jesus was first met by Martha, then Mary, who fell in anguish at His feet, the second time Scripture records Mary at Jesus's feet. When He saw Mary's anguish, Jesus was moved with compassion, and tears streamed down His face (John 11:35). He understood the pain of loss so many gathered there were feeling.

But Jesus also foresaw what was still to come. Lazarus's death was never going to be permanent. Jesus had told His disciples this very thing days earlier (John 11:4). He'd repeated it to Mary's sister Martha upon His return: "Your brother will rise and live" (John 11:23 TPT).

The miracle of Lazarus's resurrection caused many to acknowledge Jesus as the Messiah. It brought in a huge harvest of believers and revealed the greatness of the Son of God as Jesus had prophesied to His disciples days earlier. This story and so many other biblical accounts show us that our timing is not the same as God's timing. He is all-knowing and omnipresent. Where we only see in part, God sees in whole. Hindsight is what some might call it. I see it as God outside of time presenting in His perfect time.

Time was also of the essence for one hundred and twenty believers all gathered in an upper room waiting to receive the gift the Father had promised of being baptised in the Holy Spirit (Acts 1:4-5). These followers of Christ didn't know exactly when this promise would be fulfilled. Jesus had already told His disciples it wasn't for them to know the times or dates set by the Father but that they could expect to receive power when God sent His Holy Spirit. So they needed to wait patiently for God's perfect timing.

> He said to them: "It is not for you to know the times or dates the Father has set by his own authority. But you will receive power when the Holy Spirit comes on you; and you will be my witnesses in Jerusalem, and in all Judea and Samaria, and to the ends of the earth." (Acts 1:7-8)

Had the one hundred and twenty believers left the upper room where they were *abiding* in constant prayer and worship, *waiting* for the promised gift from the Father, they might have missed out on *receiving* the Holy Spirit in such a spectacular way. This group included Mary the mother of

Jesus along with other women who were devout followers of Jesus, (Acts 1:14), so Mary Magdalene and Mary of Bethany were very likely present. Since they chose to abide and wait, they received and witnessed God's miraculous timing when the Holy Spirit was finally breathed into their lives.

> Suddenly they heard the sound of a violent blast of wind rushing into the house from out of the heavenly realm. The roar of the wind was so overpowering it was all anyone could bear! Then all at once, a pillar of fire appeared before their eyes. It separated into tongues of fire that engulfed each one of them. They were all filled and equipped with the Holy Spirit and were inspired to speak in tongues—empowered by the Spirit to speak in languages they had never learned. (Acts 2:1-4 TPT)

God's timing will always bring with it something fresh and new. The Israelites experienced this when they received fresh manna every day while wandering in the wilderness (Exodus 16). They didn't have to eat stale food. Rather, God provided them with His heavenly nourishment. Similarly, when the Holy Spirit came upon those in the upper room, their lives were set ablaze with the fire of God. They were never the same again. One miraculous touch from God will have that sort of impact on a person's life.

This is something we too can receive. Our heavenly Father sets His watch over us, providing for our every need. And He sometimes does this in the most spectacular and miraculous ways as the Old Testament patriarch Job understood well. Despite all his great losses and physical suffering (Job 1), Job recognised God's omnipotence and that there is no limit to God's mysterious ways.

> Can you fathom the mysteries of God? Can you probe the limits of the Almighty? They are higher than the heavens above—what can you do? They are deeper than the depths below—what can you know? Their measure is longer than the earth and wider than the sea. (Job 11:7-9)

There is so much more that God wants to reveal to us, but He chooses the times and seasons. Scripture tells us that we only see and know in part (1 Corinthians 13:9). This means there are things that God has chosen for His purposes to conceal, awaiting His appointed time to reveal them.

> The secret things belong to the Lord our God, but the things revealed belong to us and to our children forever, that we may follow all the words of this law.
> (Deuteronomy 29:29)

Scripture tells us that even the universe is 'standing on tiptoe, yearning [waiting] to see the unveiling of God's glorious sons and daughters' (Romans 8:19 TPT). We are the sons and daughters this Scripture speaks of, and we are waiting with eager anticipation for the revelation of the return of Jesus. Scripture is riddled with God's hidden secrets, each awaiting their perfect time of release. Something I discovered more of as I will share next.

CHAPTER TWENTY-THREE

Herald The Revelation

Write down the revelation and make it plain on tablets so that a herald may run with it. For the revelation awaits an appointed time; it speaks of the end and will not prove false. Though it linger, wait for it; it will certainly come and will not delay.

—Habakkuk 2:2-3

In March 2020, God instructed me to leave my employment at a nearby Baptist church where I had been serving in multiple ministry areas for almost five years. When I handed my two-week resignation, Covid-19 restrictions and lockdowns were not yet in place in Australia, nor did we envisage what the year ahead would bring. Since God had asked me to leave that assignment, I assumed He would quickly provide whatever ministry opportunity He had planned next for me. But two weeks can bring a lot of change when the coronavirus is involved.

My city went into lockdown the day following my last day of ministry work at this Baptist church. We remained under some type of strict lockdown restrictions for most of 2020, and in fact, restrictions continued throughout Australia for much of 2021 as well. In March 2020, we began a new norm of home-schooling, businesses being shut down, and churches having to close their doors and move to online services.

This meant employment options for ministry were not readily available. Nor was I then in a position to accept new employment due to my home-schooling and other household responsibilities. As I entered this new stay-at-home season, I began a daily prayer and fasting routine, sometimes walking and talking with God for hours on end. I didn't understand initially why God had asked me to step out of ministry. All I had was a promise of His faithfulness as I stepped into unknown territory, trusting and waiting for what He wanted to do next in my life.

My faith journey was not so dissimilar to that of Abraham when he too left his homeland with only a promise of God's faithfulness.

> Faith motivated Abraham to obey God's call and leave the familiar to discover the territory he was destined to inherit from God. So he left with only a promise and without even knowing ahead of time where he was going, Abraham stepped out in faith. (Hebrews 11:8 TPT)

Mary and her husband Joseph faced a similar situation when Jesus was first born. To protect the Saviour of the world from the deadly wrath of King Herod, Mary and Joseph had to step out in faith and obey the warning they'd received from the angel of the Lord to flee to Egypt (Matthew 2:13-15).

My faith journey was far less dramatic than Mary and Joseph's. It was certainly not a matter of life or death. But it was as I stepped out in faith, leaving behind the familiarity of my previous ministry assignment, not knowing where God was taking me next, that God spoke to me about an assignment for which He was preparing me that required my abiding frequently in His presence.

I can only describe my new assignment as like being in God University. The Holy Spirit was my Lecturer, and I was His student. As we communed each day together, the Spirit of God imparted His truths to me, downloading much prophetic insight. Whatever He imparted, I wrote down. This became my daily routine.

This was not a new model God was using with me. I have been walking and talking with God for many years now. But during this particular season, it seemed far more concentrated and intense. I could sense it was an essential form of training for the ministry to which God was preparing me. And since I wanted to be trusted with *more* as Jesus describes of a good and trustworthy steward (Luke 16), I recognised the importance of stewarding this season as faithfully as I could.

It was on the first day of this God University that God's mysterious ways once again left me in awe and wonder of His goodness and mercy. That day a favourite Scripture became experiential for me.

> It is the glory of God to conceal a matter, to search out a matter is the glory of kings. (Proverbs 25:2)

This came about because God asked me on this first day of my stay-at-home season to research the creation story. This seemed an unusual topic for my first assignment. Other than the fact that we walked and talked in God's creation, I could see no reason why it would be relevant to my situation. Nevertheless when I returned home from my walk, I obediently readied myself to research the creation story.

Some two years prior, a friend had given me a Bible that has parallel translations. I had never opened that particular Bible, but on this occasion I felt compelled to use it. The moment I took the Bible off the bookshelf and opened it up, a pamphlet fell out and onto the floor. As I unfolded the pamphlet and read the headline caption, I sat stunned. The pamphlet had been published in 1991 by an organisation called Creation Ministry, and it contained a write-up all about the creation story.

I'm not entirely sure why I chose to look at the creation story through this particular Bible on that particular day. I assume the Holy Spirit spoke this idea into my spirit. But receiving this little pamphlet on creation written some twenty-nine years earlier on the very same day God had asked me to research that topic could not be coincidence.

I saw it as God reaching down to His daughter to solidify her new assignment as His student. I can visualise God's pleasure in concealing that little Creation Ministry pamphlet in my friend's Bible all those years ago. I even like to think the angels were anticipating that day I finally found this hidden treasure.

To me, it was God's way of tangibly revealing His intention for my life. It was such an encouragement to me that I was on the right path, and it gave me great assurance as I waited for God to reveal my new ministry assignment to me.

You see, sometimes as in our queen-in-waiting season, we are also in a *heralding season* as described in the Habakkuk 2 passage at the beginning of this chapter. This was certainly my assignment throughout 2020. As I received whatever revelation God desired to impart to me, I wrote it down and then heralded it, prophesying and stewarding that revelation until it came to pass. Nor in my case did it 'linger'. Just six months later, a new prophetic ministry opened up for me. I can take no credit as it was orchestrated entirely by the hand of the Almighty, one more testament of God's faithfulness to His children.

CHAPTER TWENTY-FOUR

Testify Of His Goodness

It is my pleasure to tell you about the miraculous signs and wonders that the Most High God has performed for me. How great are his signs, how mighty his wonders! His kingdom is an eternal kingdom; his dominion endures from generation to generation.

—Daniel 4:2-3

God had spoken to me in January 2020 that I would be entering into a sabbatical year of rest. A season "that will feel surreal" is how the Spirit of God explained it to me. When I received this word, I was still heavily involved in ministry. I had no idea I was soon to resign. I certainly had no notion that I would enter into a year of less 'work' but more productivity. A year of only doing what God ordained and through His promised rest. It most certainly did feel surreal as God set His watch over me, giving me a glorious reset in my ministry life.

What I've come to accept and celebrate is not just that God's timing is always perfect but that He does things with purpose in mind. When God asks us to step out in faith, He is asking us to trust that He will fulfil His perfect plan for our lives in His timing. It's not always easy to herald the revelation that 'awaits an appointed time' (Habakkuk 2:2-3). Mary, mother of Jesus, would have understood this all too well. Carrying the weight of revelation that the child she bore was in fact the Son of God, Mary had to safeguard His true identity which awaited an appointed time to be revealed. In this circumstance, Mary chose the better Mary option of *waiting* for God's perfect timing, and she chose to herald the revelation, 'treasuring all these things and pondering them in her heart' (Luke 2:19, author's paraphrase).

Throughout this book, I have mentioned many of God's beloved who have had an incredible encounter with the God of the universe. He turned up in their lives exactly at His appointed time, and this always had perfect results. My own experiences have hopefully also testified to God's perfect timing. When we go through valley seasons or a queen-in-waiting maturing process, it can sometimes feel that God is distant or not present at all. But the proof of His perfect timing is in our testimonies.

Mary Magdalene was healed at the exact time to become one of Jesus's most devout followers. She was later situated perfectly when and where she needed to be to greet the resurrected King. Esther came into her royal position for such a time as to save her people from annihilation. Moses also encountered God at a specific moment through a non-extinguishing burning bush after forty years of hiding in the wilderness, realigning his destiny and that of the Israelite nation. Jael was right where God needed her to be in her tent when God used what was in her hands for the extraordinary.

Mary of Bethany endured many days of waiting before witnessing the perfectly timed miraculous resurrections of both her brother and her Saviour. The woman with the issue of blood waited for twelve years for her *suddenly* and *then one day* moment. God used Hosea at the appointed time to redeem His daughter Gomer, reclaiming in the process God's beloved Israel back to the Father. Mary the mother to Jesus was also chosen when the exact fullness of time (Galatians 4:4) had come to bear the long-awaited Messiah.

These are just a handful of biblical precedents that encourage us to stand firm and wait for God's perfect timing in our lives. God meets us at His perfect hour because He is outside of time. Like the miraculous birth of my daughter Faith, whose arrival was the result of a promise after nine years of waiting. Like my family heirloom fob-watch that mysteriously began to tell time for one week from the day of my daughter's birth. Like the pamphlet written twenty-nine years earlier that fell out of my Bible at the perfect time to encourage my faith walk.

Each of these testimonies show us that the God of the universe invades our time not a second too late. Our testimonies proclaim God's awe and wonder. The God-moments we've experienced personally or the testimony of someone else's experience where God intervened in their life helps strengthen and stir up our faith. They encourage us to persevere when we are in a season of testing or God is refining us to steward the *more* He entrusts to us.

King David drew on the testament of his ancestors when overwhelmed with grief and fear.

> My God, my God, why have you forsaken me? Why are you so far from saving me, so far from my cries of anguish? My God, I cry out by day, but you do not answer, by night, but I find no rest. Yet you are enthroned as the Holy One; you are the one Israel praises. In you our ancestors put their trust; they trusted and you delivered them. To you they cried out and were saved; in you they trusted and were not put to shame. (Psalm 22:1-5)

Though David felt abandoned by God at that moment, he chose to draw comfort and encouragement from other people's testimonies, trusting that the God who had saved those who had gone before him would do it again. This lifted his spirit in his time of need, enabling him to once again sing praise to the King of the universe:

> I will declare your name to my people; in the assembly I will praise you. (Psalm 22:22)

Testimony is a powerful testament to God's love and goodness. In fact, Jesus Himself told His disciples that they were to testify of all that they had learned by walking with Him from the start (John 15:27). He also told them that they were to be His witness to the ends of the earth

(Acts 1:8). This included bearing witness to the miracles Jesus performed, so many that if each were written down individually, the world itself wouldn't have room to contain the books (John 21:25).

Our testimonies not only encourage and build up the body of Christ but can lead an unbeliever to Christ as well. While they can never supersede the testament of God's written Word, they speak very powerfully of the relational heart of our heavenly Father who longs to give wonderful, good, and even miraculous gifts to His children.

> If you, imperfect as you are, know how to lovingly take care of your children and give them what's best, how much more ready is your heavenly Father to give wonderful gifts to those who ask him? (Matthew 7:11 TPT)

Testimony reveals the glory and majesty of the great I Am, the Alpha and Omega, the Beginning and the End, the One Who Is and Was and Is to Come (Revelation 21:6). It demonstrates God's omnipotence and omniscience, reminding us that God is ultimately in control. God is the One who sits enthroned above the circle of the earth (Isaiah 40:22). And because of His great and unmeasurable love for us, He holds us carefully and lovingly in the palm of His hands (Psalm 95:4-7).

I truly hope you have been as blessed as I have by the testimonies of Mary of Bethany, Mary Magdalene, and Mary mother of Jesus, along with all the other men and women of the Bible I've written about throughout this book. I have loved researching their stories in light of the three Mary postures of *abiding, waiting* and *receiving*. I have found their testaments of God's faithfulness so inspiring. I have been in awe of the intricate details of our heavenly Father's miracle-working wonders in each of their lives.

I pray that Mary of Bethany's longing to just abide at the feet of Jesus, gleaning, learning, and even weeping, has encouraged you to do the same. She has certainly inspired me to desire more than anything to sit at the feet of my Master. Her testimony shows us that by His side is where we belong, and it is always the better option. As with His daughter Mary, Jesus wants to be our teacher. He desires to be our strength and source of comfort. We are all His most precious, and His love for us is extravagant.

I trust Mary Magdalene's story has also touched your heart as much as it has mine. She was 'one way' until she met Jesus, when she was completely made brand-new as *The Chosen* series scripted so beautifully. This is who we are as well, a brand-new creation in Christ, covered in His righteousness, and made perfect because of His perfection.

Mary Magdalene's story also reminds us that sometimes we will be in a queen-in-waiting season. Waiting was part of Mary's constant posture, whether on the long road to Calvary, at the tomb, or in the upper room where she received the Holy Spirit. Waiting for God's perfect timing is not always easy but will always produce the best results.

And then there is Mary, mother to Jesus and 'most blessed among all women' (Luke 1:42, author's paraphrase). Just as God chose and appointed Mary for this special assignment, He knew and appointed us with destiny in His mind even before forming us in our mother's womb (Ephesians 1:11). He has a perfect plan for each of us that He longs to reveal so we can walk out our destiny with Jesus leading the way. We are all purposed with God-assignments. There are no exceptions. And to carry out His plan in our lives, He makes the ordinary into the extraordinary.

So, as I conclude my writings on these three Marys, I pray that you have been inspired by their stories as well as many others. I also hope that my own testimony of spending time communing with my Papa encourages you to spend time being *present* in His *presence* as well. Whether in your secret chamber or on a hilltop or having 'a cuppa with your Papa' as have been my own intimate experiences with God, our heavenly Father is inviting all of His children to commune with Him and enjoy our very own Mount Sinai encounter sanctuary, wherever and whatever that looks like to you.

We each host God's presence the moment we unite our lives with Jesus, so there is no prejudice when it comes to a relationship with God. He just wants us to come and enjoy intimate fellowship in His company. As I've said throughout this book, the Garden of Eden is our heritage. This doesn't mean we will ever return to the garden physically. A new heavenly city, the new Jerusalem, awaits us instead (Revelation 21:2). But intimate communion with our heavenly Father such as Adam and Eve enjoyed in the Garden of Eden has been part of our make-up since the beginning of time.

So, God in His triune nature is inviting us, wooing

us even as a Bridegroom, to come and partake of Him by simply *abiding, waiting,* and *receiving* directly from Him. Jesus is calling out our names as He called out Mary's name when first He arose from the grave. He is inviting us to come and walk and talk with Him in the cool of our day!

Final Exhortation

In love he chose us before he laid the foundation of the universe! Because of his great love, he ordained us, so that we would be seen as holy in his eyes with an unstained innocence. For it was always in his perfect plan to adopt us as his delightful children, through our union with Jesus, the Anointed One, so that his tremendous love that cascades over us would glorify his grace – for the same love he has for the Beloved, Jesus, he has for us. And this unfolding plan brings him great pleasure.
—Ephesians 1:4-6 TPT

DEVOTION OF MY HEART

On God-Assignment

Forever I'd only ever considered Jesus's words about the days of Noah in Matthew 24 as a warning of how in the last days people will go on living their lives, eating, drinking, marrying, and having children until it is too late. People didn't heed Noah's prophesy of a coming flood nor realise the end was nigh until Noah entered the ark and God shut the door.

But recently, God has been showing me this passage from Noah's perspective. During those final days on the Earth as he knew it, Noah was working on a God-Assignment. God had handpicked Noah for an important mission, and he remained focused on carrying out his God-given destiny with purpose and mission in mind right up until the door to the ark was closed.

There was nothing easy about the assignment with which Noah was tasked. Others mocked him and criticised and considered him fanatical. But Noah's appointment resulted in God's covenant promise for all of mankind. And by God's great love, Noah and his family were protected inside the ark.

In our generation as well, God is calling for the Noahs of our day to rise up. We have all been destined with mission in mind, and as in the days of Noah, God has an assignment for each of us as well. Knowing and then receiving our God-assignments may require faith and radical obedience. Noah experienced both. But as he also discovered, walking out our destiny with Jesus leading the way will secure us safely inside the ark of God's unending love.

EPILOGUE

Love Letters

Before we were even born, he gave us our destiny; that we would fulfil the plan of God who always accomplishes every purpose and plan in his heart.
—Ephesians 1:11 TPT

Thank you for journeying with me through the pages of *In The Cool Of The Day*. I hope that through the testimonies I have shared along with God's inspired Word—His *Love Letters* written directly to us—you have been assured there is nothing that can separate us from the extravagant love of our heavenly Father. When we abide in Jesus, He has secured and covered us in His righteousness, and we can now live in the freedom of God's boundless love forevermore.

Whether this is new revelation for you or simply reaffirming what you already know, it is the heart of the Father for all of us to know how deeply and far-reaching His love is for His dearly beloved. We are Jesus's glorious and radiant bride. We are also His friend, partner, and co-heir to the kingdom of heaven. We are His precious darlings in whom He delights and to whom we are flawless and beautiful in our Bridegroom's eyes.

We are also His most highly-favoured and beautiful

ones, created in the image of God and destined with purpose for His pleasure. His *Love Letters* remind us over and again of just how captivated our King is towards His beloved.

God's perfect love is truly a great mystery. One day that mystery will be revealed to us in its entirety. For now, it is too great to fully understand (Ephesians 3:18-19). But when the day arrives for us to dwell forever in the presence of our Lord, we will know the completeness of His love.

Until then, we can still enjoy being loved and loving our King in return. This book is devoted to *walking and talking with God in the cool of our day* (Genesis 3:8). It is our destiny to commune intimately with our heavenly Father as we've examined in depth through the three Mary postures of *abiding, waiting,* and *receiving*. God yearns for relationship with His children, and He longs to impart His revelation-secrets to us so we can walk out our destiny according to His perfect plan and purpose.

Jesus said that as it was in Noah's day, so shall it be in the last days before He returns (Matthew 24:37-39). This means that like Noah we are all on God-assignment right now until the very end of our days. Whether we are walking out our destiny already or God is yet to reveal the plans He has for you, we have all been co-missioned for such a time as to partner with our Bridegroom, Jesus. Even if like Noah our assignments require radical faith and obedience, we can rest assured they will be wrapped in God's pure and perfect love. And God's protection of Noah and his family inside the ark of God's love is a foreshadowing for us of the ark of salvation found only through Jesus.

I could go on and on about destiny as it is so dear to my heart to see God's beloved walk out their destiny according to the riches of His grace. But for now, I want to leave you with this final exhortation through Solomon's poetic, intimate words of love spoken allegorically from our beloved Bridegroom.

The entire book of Song of Songs illustrates Christ's deep desire to spend intimate time with His beloved. He calls for His bride to draw closer and come away with Him to higher grounds so He can whisper new revelatory mysteries to us.

It speaks of a budding new destiny that is bursting forth within His bride. It paints a beautiful picture of the extravagant love our Bridegroom has for us. It is another of God's glorious *Love Letters*, so I hope it encourages you one final time to *abide, wait,* and *receive* from your beautiful One—Jesus.

> Arise, my dearest. Hurry, my darling. Come away with me! I have come as you have asked to draw you to my heart and lead you out. For now is the time, my beautiful one. The season has changed, the bondage of your barren winter has ended, and the season of hiding is over and gone. The rains have soaked the earth and left it bright with blossoming flowers. The season for singing and pruning the vines has arrived. I hear the cooing of doves in our land, filling the air with songs to awaken you and guide you forth. Can you not discern this new day of destiny breaking forth around you? The early signs of my purposes and plans are bursting

forth. The budding vines of new life are now blooming everywhere. The fragrance of their flowers whispers, "There is change in the air". Arise, my love, my beautiful companion, and run with me to the higher place. For now is the time to arise and come away with me.
(Song of Songs 2:10-13 TPT)

In His extravagant love,

Nicole

www.nicolezoch.com

APPENDIX

ETERNAL LIFE

If you declare with your mouth, "Jesus is Lord," and believe in your heart that God raised him from the dead, you will be saved. For it is with your heart that you believe and are justified, and it is with your mouth that you profess your faith and are saved.

—Romans 10:9-10

Having a relationship with Jesus Christ changed my life. It can change yours too. If you haven't yet entered into a personal relationship with God the Father, His Son, and His Spirit, I encourage you to take this important step in your life. As the Scripture passage above makes clear, it is as simple as inviting Jesus into your life, confessing Him as your Lord, and believing He is the Son of God. Here is an example of a simple salvation prayer you can pray.

Prayer for Salvation

Lord Jesus, I come to You with a repentant heart, asking for the forgiveness of my sins. Thank you for dying on the cross for me and taking away all my sins. By Your blood offering, I am now cleansed today and forever. I thank the Father for sending You. I believe You are the Son of God who died on the cross, rose again, and is now seated at the right hand of our Father, preparing a home for me in heaven. I love You, Lord Jesus, and I thank You, Father, for sending the Holy Spirit to us after Jesus ascended into heaven. I give You my life and thank You for giving me eternal life. Amen.

Nurturing Your Christian Walk

Once you have prayed this prayer, dear reader, I would also encourage you to start reading the Bible, the living Word of God. The Bible is where truth will be revealed as Jesus Himself stated:

I am the way and the truth and the life. (John 14:6)
The truth will set you free. (John 8:32)

To be nurtured in your Christian walk, it is also important to find a Bible-believing, Christ-centred, Spirit-filled church family who can journey alongside you. It is very difficult to live out faith alone, so I truly encourage you to find someone who shares your faith beliefs who can journey this season with you.

ABOUT THE AUTHOR

With all my heart and passion I will thank you, my God! I will give glory to your name, always and forever.

—Psalm 86:12 TPT

Nicole Zoch resides in the countryside of Victoria, Australia with her husband Jamie, and three children, Faith, Joel, and Levi. Nicole has been in church ministry for over twenty years, including most recently as the Lead Elder/Prophet in a five-fold ministry church modelled on Christ's ascension gifts as described in Ephesians 4:11. She currently co-leads a *mobile* House of Prayer/Healing Ministry, ministering wherever the Holy Spirit leads their team. Nicole is also a passionate encourager through her writing and prophetic teaching.

Whilst passionate about equipping God's beloved to walk out their God-given purpose and calling, Nicole also has a desire to see the broken-hearted restored, and to encourage others to accept their true worth and value in Christ. This passion was birthed after Nicole and Jamie came out of a legalistic church upbringing and tried to do life their way. It ended up messy! It was the *unlikely gift* of a nine-year infertility-to-motherhood journey that led Nicole on a restorative faith path of her own.

As she desperately sought answers for her empty womb, God began to reveal more of Himself to her;

drawing Nicole deeper into an intimate relationship with the Trinity of God. As she describes in her first book, *Having Faith: One Woman's Nine-Year Faith Journey from Infertility to Motherhood,* it was out of this extraordinary faith journey that Nicole learned to extravagantly worship, trust, and desire God more than anything else. The love of the Lord permeated deep within her heart and soul from that moment on, and Nicole's life was wonderfully and forevermore changed.

To contact Nicole for prayer, speaking engagements, or to purchase her books, please visit her Author Page: https://www.nicolezoch.com